Second Edition

Syrian Refugee Guide to Canada

Revised and Updated

2017

By Barbara Dixon
Diversity ERAA Training
Winnipeg, Manitoba, Canada
Email: diversityeraa.com

ISBN-13: 978-1543094435

ISBN-10:1543094430

INTRODUCTION

Welcome to Canada!

The *Syrian Refugee Guide to Canada* highlights the most important information newcomers need to know to successfully settle in Canada and integrate into the Canadian workplace.

The *Syrian Refugee Guide to Canada* is also a useful tool for private sponsors, settlement workers and employers. It provides comprehensive information on what Syrian refugees need to know to make an easy transition to life in their new home country.

The *Syrian Refugee Guide to Canada* is divided into six chapters:
Chapter 1: Pre-Arrival - Learning about Canada
Chapter 2: Coping with Culture Shock and Trauma
Chapter 3: Settlement and Integration
Chapter 4: Find a Job
Chapter 5: Cultural Differences
Chapter 6: Canadian Workplace Culture

Barbara Dixon is available to help immigrants and refugees be successful. Consultation services and training is available to both newcomers and employers. Contact Barbara directly at: **diversityeraa@gmail.com** or through Diversity ERAA Training's website: **http://diversityeraa.ca**

I hope you will find this *Guide* helpful!
Barbara Dixon
Senior Consultant and President, Diversity ERAA Training
Winnipeg, Manitoba, Canada

CONTENTS

CHAPTER 1: ARRIVAL

CHAPTER 2: COPING WITH CULTURE SHOCK

CHAPTER 3: SETTLEMENT AND INTEGRATION

CHAPTER 4: FIND A JOB

CHAPTER 5: CULTURAL DIFFERENCES

CHAPTER 6: CANADIAN WORKPLACE CULTURE

APPENDICES

CHAPTER 1: ARRIVAL

Challenges and opportunities lie ahead when you arrive in Canada.

As a government sponsored refugee or as a private sponsored refugee, you will be located where the government initially designates or where your sponsors live.

As a Permanent Resident of Canada, you have the same rights of mobility as Canadians. What this means is that you can move to wherever you want to live in Canada or where you find a job.

This section is designed to help ease the transition of moving to Canada.

Learn About Canada

Canada is a very large country. There are ten provinces and three territories. There are six time zones. Canada is much more than Toronto, Vancouver or Montreal. Have you ever heard of Winnipeg, Saskatoon, Edmonton, Ottawa or Halifax? These are just some of the other major cities, which you could choose to live in.

Remember to choose a destination where jobs exist in your field and where the cost of living is affordable to you.

Canada's West Coast Province: British Columbia

British Columbia is Canada's westernmost province and is set between the Pacific Ocean in the west and the province of Alberta and the Rocky Mountains in the east. According to Statistics Canada, 17.6% of Canada's immigrants live in British Columbia.[1] The cost of living in British Columbia depends on where you choose to live.

The capital of British Columbia is Victoria. It is located on the southern tip of Vancouver Island. Victoria is a medium-sized city. A high proportion of the labour force works in public administration, tourism and retail trade.[2] Victoria has pleasant weather, particularly during winter and has become a popular retirement destination. Local purchasing power in Victoria is 1.38% lower than in Toronto.[3]

For many newcomers, the only city they know of in British Columbia is Vancouver. Vancouver is Canada's 8th largest city. Major economic sectors include film, international commerce and trade, natural resources, technology and tourism.[4] Local purchasing power in Vancouver is 29.94% lower than in Toronto.[5]

---

[1] Statistics Canada, http://www12.statcan.gc.ca/nhs-enm/2011/as-sa/99-010-x/99-010-x2011001-eng.cfm

[2] Work BC, https://www.workbc.ca/Statistics/Labour-Market.aspx

[3] Numbeo, http://www.numbeo.com/cost-of-living/compare_cities.jsp?country1=Canada&country2=Canada&city1=Toronto&city2=Victoria

[4] Ibid

[5] Numbeo, http://www.numbeo.com/cost-of-living/compare_cities.jsp?country1=Canada&country2=Canada&city1=Toronto&city2=Vancouver

Vancouver, British Columbia

Vancouver is the most expensive city in Canada to live. Demographia International Housing Affordability 2016 Survey ranked Vancouver as the second most unaffordable housing market in the world after Hong Kong.[6] Choosing to live in a different city or a smaller community in British Columbia will offer you a lower cost of living.

Other cities to consider living in British Columbia include: Armstrong, Burnaby, Campbell River, Castlegar, Chilliwack, Colwood, Coquitlam, Courtenay, Cranbrook, Dawson Creek, Enderby, Fernie, Fort St. John, Grand Forks, Kamloops, Kelowna, Kimberley, Langford, Langley, Maple Ridge, Merritt, Nanaimo, Nelson, New Westminster, North Vancouver, Parksville, Penticton, Pitt Meadows, Port Alberni, Port Coquitlam, Port moody,

[6] 11th Annual Demographia International Housing Affordability Survey: 2016, http://www.demographia.com/dhi.pdf

Powell River, Prince George, Prince Rupert, Quesnel, Revelstoke, Richmond, Rossland, Salmon Arm, Surrey, Terrace, Trail, Vernon, White Rock and Williams Lake.

According to the Conference Board of Canada, British Columbia's economic growth will slow in 2017 due to a pullback in the booming housing sector.[7]

Immigration Portal for British Columbia: https://www.welcomebc.ca/home.aspx

Canada's Prairie Provinces: Alberta, Saskatchewan and Manitoba

The three Prairie Provinces from west to east are: Alberta, Saskatchewan and Manitoba. According to Statistics Canada, 9.5% of Canada's immigrants live in Alberta, 5.0% in Manitoba and 2.3% in Saskatchewan. [8]

Alberta

Alberta has many cost of living advantages compared to the average cost of living in Canada. It is the only province in Canada with no provincial sales tax, the lowest tax on gasoline, and it has some of the lowest property taxes in the country.

Alberta's capital is Edmonton. Edmonton is Canada's 5th largest city. Finance, real estate, trade, professional, technical and

---

[7] Conference Board of Canada, http://www.conferenceboard.ca/e-library/abstract.aspx?did=8522

[8] Ibid

management services and manufacturing are primary industries in Edmonton. [9]

In 2016, Edmonton was named the 7th best large city to live in Canada.[10] Local purchasing power in Edmonton is 6.36% lower than in Toronto.[11]

Calgary is Canada's 3rd largest city by both population and area. Calgary is the major centre for the global energy industry. Other prospective employers exist in the technology sector, finance and business services, manufacturing, transportation and logistics, film and creative industries.[12] Local purchasing power in Calgary is 3.02% higher than in Toronto. [13]

St Albert was considered to be the best place to live in Alberta in 2016.[14] Other cities to consider living in Alberta include: Airdrie, Brooks, Camrose, Cherstermere, Cold Lake, Fort Saskatchewan, Grande Prairie, Lacombe, Leduc, Lethbridge, Lloydminster, Medicine Hat, red deer, Spruce Grove, and Wetaskiwin.

According to the Conference Board of Canada, no further major cuts to energy investment are forecast. However, the number of unemployed Albertans will remain higher compared to recent years due to cutbacks in the oil industry.[15]

---

[9] The City of Edmonton, http://www.edmonton.ca/business_economy/demographics_profiles/industries.aspx
[10] MoneySense, http://www.moneysense.ca/canadas-best-places-to-live-2016-full-ranking/
[11] Numbeo, ,http://www.numbeo.com/cost-of-living/compare_cities.jsp?country1=Canada&country2=Canada&city1=Toronto&city2=Edmonton
[12] Calgary Economic Development, http://www.calgaryeconomicdevelopment.com/industries
[13] Numbeo,http://www.numbeo.com/cost-of-living/compare_cities.jsp?country1=Canada&country2=Canada&city1=Toronto&city2=Calgary
[14] MoneySense, http://www.moneysense.ca/save/financial-planning/canadas-best-places-to-live-2016-overview/
[15] Conference Board of Canada, http://www.conferenceboard.ca/e-library/abstract.aspx?did=8521

Saskatchewan

The cost of living in Saskatchewan is considered low compared to the rest of Canada. The provincial sales tax is 5% and is the lowest of the nine provinces that charge a sales tax. Housing costs are lower in Saskatchewan than in most major cities in Canada making it affordable to own a home.

Regina is Saskatchewan's capital city. It is the 2nd largest city in Saskatchewan and is the province's finance and insurance centre. Agribusiness, steel and manufacturing, information technology, energy and environment, finance and insurance, and real estate are some other major industries in Regina. Local purchasing power in Regina is 1.91 % lower than in Toronto.[16]

Saskatoon is the largest city by both population and area. It is considered to be a medium-sized city and is one Canada's fastest growing cities. Primary industries include agriculture, mining, oil and gas, transportation and logistics. Local purchasing power in Saskatoon is 18.41% lower than in Toronto.[17]

In 2016, Weyburn was considered the best city to live in Saskatchewan.[18] Other cities to consider living in include: Estevan, Flin Flon, Humboldt, Lloydminster, Meadow Lake, Martensville,

---

[16]Numbeo, http://www.numbeo.com/cost-of-living/compare_cities.jsp?country1=Canada&country2=Canada&city1=Toronto&city2=Regina
[17] Numbeo, http://www.numbeo.com/cost-of-living/compare_cities.jsp?country1=Canada&country2=Canada&city1=Toronto&city2=Saskatoon
[18] MoneySense, http://www.moneysense.ca/spend/real-estate/canadas-best-places-to-live-2016-prairies/

Melfort, Melville, Moose Jaw, North Battleford, Prince Albert, Swift Current, Warman and Yorkton.

Immigration Portal Saskatchewan: www.saskatchewan.ca/residents/moving-to-saskatchewan/immigrating-to-saskatchewan

Manitoba

Manitoba is one of the most affordable provinces in Canada. House prices, car insurance, utilities, and post-secondary tuition costs are some of the lowest costs in Canada. Manitoba continually has one of the lowest unemployment rates in Canada.

Manitoba's capital is Winnipeg. It is Canada's 7th largest city and Manitoba's largest city even though it is considered to be medium-sized.

In 2016, Winnipeg was named the 3rd best large city to live in Canada.[19] Sales and service, business, finance and administration, medical research, and logistics, trade and transportation are the major industries with employment.[20] Local purchasing power in Winnipeg is 21.61% lower than in Toronto.[21]

Brandon is the 2nd largest city in Manitoba. The majority of employment in Brandon is in the health care, social services,

---

[19] MoneySense, http://www.moneysense.ca/canadas-best-places-to-live-2016-full-ranking/

[21] Numbeo, http://www.numbeo.com/cost-of-living/compare_cities.jsp?country1=Canada&country2=Canada&city1=Toronto&city2=Winnipeg

manufacturing and retail trade.[22] Local purchasing power in Brandon is 73.46% lower than in Toronto.[23]

Hillside Beach, Manitoba

Dauphin is Manitoba's smallest city by area and Flin Flon is smallest by population. Other cities to consider living in Manitoba include: Morden, Portage la Prairie, Selkirk, Steinbach, Thompson and Winkler.

According to the Conference Board of Canada, Manitoba's economy will be the second strongest in 2017.[24]

Immigration Portal for Manitoba: www.immigratemanitoba.com

[22] Economic Development Brandon, http://economicdevelopmentbrandon.com/industry-employment-business

[23] Numbeo, https://www.numbeo.com/cost-of-living/compare_cities.jsp?country1=Canada&country2=Canada&city1=Toronto&city2=Brandon%2C+MB

[24] http://globalnews.ca/news/2564025/manitobas-economy-among-strongest-in-country-conference-board-of-canada/

Central Canada: Ontario and Quebec

Central Canada refers to Canada's two largest and most populous provinces, Ontario and Quebec. According to Statistics Canada, 53.3% of Canada's immigrants live in Ontario and 14.4% of Canada's immigrants live in Quebec.[25]

Parliament Building, Ottawa

Ontario

Ontario's capital and Canada's largest city is Toronto. The key industry sectors are business and professional services, design, education, fashion, film and television, finance environmental, life sciences, music, tourism and hospitality, and technology.[26]

Ottawa is Canada's capital and 4th largest city. It is a medium-sized city. In 2017, Ottawa-Gatineau was listed as Canada's most affordable major housing market. However, it was still considered to be moderately unaffordable.[27]

---

[25] Statistics Canada, http://www12.statcan.gc.ca/nhs-enm/2011/as-sa/99-010-x/99-010-x2011001-eng.cfm

[26] City of Toronto, *Key Industry Sectors*, http://www1.toronto.ca/wps/portal/contentonly?vgnextoid=401132d0b6d1e310VgnVCM10000071d60f89RCRD

[27] 13th Annual Demographia International housing Affordability Survey: 2017, https://fcpp.org/wp-content/uploads/Final-Demographia-2017.pdf

Public administration and high technology are the primary sectors in Ottawa.[28] Local purchasing power in Ottawa is 10.79% higher than Toronto.[29]

St. Catherines – Port Weller, Lock 3

Mississauga is Canada's 6th largest city. Brampton is Canada's 9th largest city and Hamilton is Canada's 10th largest city. Hamilton, Kitchener, London, Oshawa, St. Catherines, Windsor and Sudbury are all considered to be medium-sized cities.

Other cities to consider living in Ontario include: Barrie, Belleville, Brampton, Brant, Brantford, Brockville, Burlington, Cambridge, Clarence-Rockland, Cornwall, Elliot Lake, Guelph, Haldimand County, Kawartha Lakes, Kenora, Kingston, Kitchener, London,

[28] City of Ottawa, *Economy and Demographics*, http://ottawa.ca/en/long-range-financial-plans/long-range-financial-plan-iii-part-1-and-part-2/economy-and-demographics
[29] Numbeo, http://www.numbeo.com/cost-of-living/compare_cities.jsp?country1=Canada&country2=Canada&city1=Toronto&city2=Ottawa

Markham, Niagara Falls, Norfolk County, North Bay, Orillia, Oshawa, Owen Sound, Peterborough, Pickering, Port Colbourne, Prince Edward County, Quinte West, Sarnia, Sault Ste. Marie, St. Catherines, St. Thomas, Stratford, Temiskaming Shores, Thorold, Thunder Bay, Timmins, Vaughan, Waterloo, Welland, Windsor and Woodstock.

Niagara Falls, Ontario

Immigration Portal for Ontario:
www.ontarioimmigration.ca

Quebec

Quebec's capital is Quebec City. It is Quebec's 2nd largest city and was ranked in 2016 as the 2nd best large city to live in.[30]

Montreal is Canada's 2nd largest city and Quebec's largest city by population.

---

[30] MoneySense, http://www.moneysense.ca/canadas-best-places-to-live-2015-full-ranking/

The key industries in Quebec are ICT and electronics, life sciences, food processing, insurance and financial services, green and smart building and value-added materials and transportation equipment.[31]

Immigration Portal for Quebec:
http://www.immigration-
quebec.gouv.qc.ca/fr/index.php

Atlantic Provinces: New Brunswick, Nova Scotia, Prince Edward Island and Newfoundland and Labrador

Canada's Atlantic provinces from west to east include: New Brunswick, Nova Scotia, Prince Edward Island and Newfoundland and Labrador. According to Statistics Canada, 0.5% of Canadian immigrants live in New Brunswick, 0.9% live in Nova Scotia, 0.2% live in Prince Edward Island and 0.2% live in Newfoundland and Labrador.[32]

New Brunswick

New Brunswick is Canada's only official bilingual (French and English) province. The three biggest cities in New Brunswick are Fredericton, Moncton and Saint John.

---

[31] Quebec International, http://www.quebecinternational.ca/key-industries
[32] Statistics Canada, http://www12.statcan.gc.ca/nhs-enm/2011/as-sa/99-010-x/99-010-x2011001-eng.cfm

The capital city of New Brunswick is Fredericton. Major industries in Fredericton include public administration, education, information technology, engineering and environmental technologies.[33]

Saint John is New Brunswick's largest city by population and area. The major industries include oil and gas, transport/distribution, electricity, brewing and call centres.[34]

Moncton is a growing high technology and service industry city.[35] In 2017, Moncton was considered to have the most affordable housing market in Canada.[36]

Immigration Portal for New Brunswick: www.gnb.ca/Immigration

Nova Scotia

The capital of Nova Scotia is Halifax. Halifax is the largest municipality city by area in Nova Scotia. Halifax harbor is the world's 2nd largest harbor. The major industries in Halifax include aerospace, health care, education, skilled trades and digital industries.[37] Local purchasing power in Halifax is 19.29% lower than in Toronto.[38]

---

[33] City of Fredericton, http://www.fredericton.ca/en/communityculture/communityprofile.asp
[34] http://foundlocally.com/stjohns/Local/Info-CityInfo.htm
[35] Living in Canada, living in New Brunswick, http://www.livingin-canada.com/living-in-new-brunswick.html
[36] 13th Annual Demographia International Housing Affordability Survey: 2017, https://fcpp.org/wp-content/uploads/Final-Demographia-2017.pdf

[37] http://twosmallmen.com/halifax-ns-movers/main-industries-and-job-opportunities-in-halifax
[38] Numbeo, http://www.numbeo.com/cost-of-living/compare_cities.jsp?country1=Canada&country2=Canada&city1=Toronto&city2=Halifax

Halifax Harbour, Nova Scotia

Immigration Portal for Nova Scotia:
www.novascotiaimmigration.ca

Prince Edward Island

Prince Edward Island is Canada's smallest province. Its capital is
Charlottetown. The main employers in Charlottetown are in sales
and service occupations, business, finance and administration and
trades.[39] Summerside is the other city in Prince Edward Island.

Immigration Portal for Prince Edward Island:
www.gov.pe.ca/immigration

---

[39] http://www.city-data.com/canada/Charlottetown-City-work.html

14

Newfoundland and Labrador

Newfoundland and Labrador is the 16th largest island in the world. The capital of Newfoundland and Labrador is St. John's, a medium-sized city.

St. John's is the largest city in Newfoundland and Labrador. Industry sectors include oil and gas, hydro, ocean technology, construction, education, culture and tourism.[40] Local purchasing power in St. John's is 21.82% lower than in Toronto.[41]

Immigration Portal for Newfoundland and Labrador: www.nlimmigration.ca

Northern Territories: Yukon, Northwest Territories and Nunavut

Canada has three northern territories: Yukon, Northwest Territories and Nunavut. The capital city of Yukon is Whitehorse. The capital of Northwest Territories is Yellowknife. The capital of Nunavut is Iqaluit.

Immigration Portal for Yukon: www.immigration.gov.yk.ca

Immigration Portal for Northwest Territories: www.gov.nt.ca

Immigration Portal for Nunavut: www.gov.nu.ca

---

[40] The Canadian Trade Commissioner Service, *St. John's: An Emerging Economy and Cultural Capital,* http://www.international.gc.ca/investors-investisseurs/cities-villes/saint_johns.aspx?lang=eng
[41] Numbeo, http://www.numbeo.com/cost-of-living/compare_cities.jsp?country1=Canada&country2=Canada&city1=Toronto&city2=St.+John%27s%2C+NL

Canadian Cities Compared

> **According to the 2011 National Household Survey, Canada's foreign-born population was 6.8 million.[1] This means that one in every five people living in Canada is an immigrant.**

Canadian cities vary in size and population. As a sponsored refugee, you have been re-located to an area of Canada where your sponsors live. Remember, you have freedom of mobility in Canada, which means you can live anywhere in Canada.

Once your sponsorship ends, you will want to live in a place where you can find a good job with affordable housing.

Many newcomers to Canada move to the Toronto area or Vancouver. Why do they choose Toronto and Vancouver as their destination? Have you ever thought about this?

Ask yourself if someone were immigrating to your Syria prior to the war, where would they plan to live? Most likely, it would be a place they had heard of or visited. This is the same reason many immigrants choose Toronto and Vancouver. They have heard of these two cities and may not know much about the rest of Canada.

City	Vancouver	Edmonton	Winnipeg	Toronto
Pop (2015)[42]	2.5 million	1.4 million	793 thousand	6 million
Foreign Born[43]	40.0%	20.4%	20.6%	46.0%
Unemployment (Dec 2016)[44]	5.1%	7.0%	6.9%	6.4%
Median Income (2014)[45]	$76,040	$101,470	$79,850	$75,270
Average House Price (Dec 2016)[46]	$948,246	$357,916	$279,651	$730,472

Canada's largest cities include: Toronto, Montreal and Vancouver. You can see, that the cost of housing in Toronto and Vancouver is much higher than other cities. If you want to purchase a house in Canada versus rent an apartment, this is something to consider.

There are many other cities and towns to choose to live in Canada. Do not make the mistake of just choosing a place you have heard of in Canada. Keep your options open when your sponsorship ends.

[42] Statistics Canada, foreign born population of cities in Canada, http://www.statcan.gc.ca/tables-tableaux/sum-som/l01/cst01/demo05a-eng.htm
[43] Statistics Canada, http://www12.statcan.gc.ca/nhs-enm/2011/as-sa/fogs-spg/Pages/CMACASelector.cfm?lang=E&level=3
[44] Statistics Canada, http://www.statcan.gc.ca/tables-tableaux/sum-som/l01/cst01/labor35-eng.htm
[45] Statistics Canada, *Median Total Income, by Family Type, By Census Metropolitan Areas*, http://www.statcan.gc.ca/tables-tableaux/sum-som/l01/cst01/famil107a-eng.htm
[46] The Canadian Real Estate Association, *National Average Price Map*, http://crea.ca/content/national-average-price-map

> **Do not just choose a place based on a higher income because this often means the cost of living is also higher.**

Medium-sized cities include: Victoria, Edmonton, Calgary, Saskatoon, Regina, Winnipeg, Sudbury, Windsor, London, Kitchener, St. Catherines, Hamilton, Oshawa, Quebec City, Halifax and St. John's.

Small-sized cities include: Kelowna, Red Deer, Moose Jaw, Brandon, Moncton, Sydney, Charlottetown and Corner Brook.

What are Canada's best cities for jobs and affordable housing? As of July 2016 here are the top ten:[47]

1. Regina, Saskatchewan
2. Edmonton, Alberta
3. Windsor, Ontario
4. Trois-Rivieres, Quebec
5. Halifax, Nova Scotia
6. Kingston, Ontario
7. Winnipeg, Manitoba
8. Oshawa, Ontario
9. St. John's, Newfoundland
10. Kitchener-Waterloo, Ontario

Canada is a very large country. There are many towns of various sizes and rural areas where you can also choose to live.

---

[47] http://www.huffingtonpost.ca/2016/07/12/best-cities-jobs-affordable-homes_n_10740892.html

Look at a map of Canada. Do research to find out about the geography of the different areas. For example, if your family enjoys going to the beach, choose a place where there is easy access to a lake or ocean.

Find out where jobs in your profession exist by learning about the labour market in Canada. For example if you are an IT specialist, where are IT specialist jobs found in Canada? If you were a restaurant owner, where is the best place to set-up a new restaurant in Canada? Do not just automatically choose a place you have heard of.

Explore the different regions of Canada to see what suits the lifestyle you want when you live here. For example, if you want to purchase a house, research the cost of housing across Canada to see which are the most affordable places to live.

Once your sponsorship ends, do not just choose to live in a place because your family or friends live there.

Where your family and friends live, may not be the place where you can find a job in your profession or where you can find affordable housing.

Comparing Canada's Population and Age[48]

	Canada	Syria
Population	36 million	22.985 million
Land Area	9,984,670 km²	186,475 km²
Population Density[49]	4 people per km²	121 people per km²
Median Age	41.8 years	23.33 years

Most people live in the southern part of Canada. Even knowing this, you have a very large area from which to choose from in terms of where you want to live. Conduct research to find the best place for you.

You will notice that there are not as many people. Initially, for some of you, this might make you feel lonely. For some, you will immediately enjoy being in a less crowded place.

You will also notice that Canadians have a larger older population than Syria and fewer children. As of the 2011 Census, the average number of children at home per family was 1.1[50].

Given Canada's aging population, your children and you will have job opportunities as the Canadian workforce retires.

---

[48] https://www.cia.gov and http://data.worldbank.org/indicator/SP.POP.TOTL
[49] http://www.indexmundi.com/g/r.aspx?v=21000
[50] http://www.statcan.gc.ca/tables-tableaux/sum-som/l01/cst01/famil50a-eng.htm

Weather

Canada has four seasons: Spring (starts March 21), Summer (starts June 21), Autumn/Fall (starts September 21) and Winter (starts December 21).

Winter officially lasts three months, but in reality, depending on where you live in Canada, is about 5 months long.

Most newcomers worry about how they will adjust to the cold weather. Your first winter will be your worst and your best. Most of you have never experienced the freezing temperatures that exist in Canada during winter. The key to enjoying winter is to stay active and wear the appropriate clothing.

Playing in the snow

All buildings and vehicles are heated during the winter. You will be warm when you are indoors.

However, it is extremely important that you stay active and get outside during the winter. Otherwise, you can become depressed and isolated. Learn how to ice skate or snowboard or ski or join a curling team. Take your children tobogganing (a sled that you sit on and go down a hill).

It is also important to maintain adequate levels of Vitamin D during winter months due to the lack of exposure to sunshine. From September 1 to June 30, you should take a minimum of 1000 International Units (IU) daily. Ask your doctor for the recommended dosage for you.

Dress for Winter

Dressing appropriately for the weather is extremely important! Your skin can freeze depending on the temperature and wind chill.

Here are some tips on how to dress in winter.

Layer Your Clothes

The best way to keep warm during winter is to layer your clothes. Start with a base, such as long underwear (sometimes referred to as long johns) or leggings and then add a few mid-layers topped with a wind-proof shell. Buy a coat that falls below the waist, preferably between your bottom and your knees. Pay the extra money to buy a good pair of winter boots. Add more layers depending on the outdoor activity.

When buying winter clothes, look for warm materials such as wool, fleece or thick synthetics. For coats, look for thinsulate or down linings. Avoid wearing cotton in winter as it can draw heat away from your body. Remember that loose clothing provides more insulation.

Remember to Cover Your Head, Ears, Neck, Hands and Feet

It is extremely important to cover your head, ears, neck, hands and feet during winter. These extremities can easily become frostbitten (injured by freezing or partial freezing). It is also very important to keep from getting wet during winter. So for example, if your children are playing in the snow, they may need to change their mittens once they get wet.

Head and Ears

In cold weather, we lose most of our body heat through our heads. Wear a wool hat or toque that covers your ears. In Canada, a toque (pronounced tuke) is another way of saying winter hat.

Neck

Buy and wear scarves that are woolen, thick and broad. You can use scarves to cover your small children's nose, mouth and top of forehead when they are playing outside.

Hands

Wear gloves or mittens that are made of wool or are insulated and covered with leather.

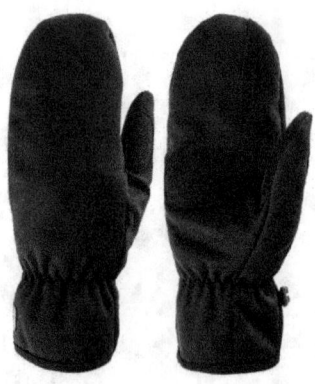

Feet

Buy a good pair of boots that are temperature rated and have a good grip on the bottom. Good quality boots costs approximately $200 for adults and about $80 for children. As you get accustomed to winter, you can then buy fashion boots. Wear winter socks that are made of wool or fleece. Be careful that your feet are comfortable in your boots and that the circulation is not constricted.

Winter can be fun if you are prepared and dress for it. Go outside! Learn to skate or ski or snowboard.

It is very important to stay active during the winter.

Explore winter and all its wonders!

Understand Wind Chill

In Canada, weather is a daily topic of conversation. People will check the weather forecast several times a day as the weather can change dramatically.

In the winter, you need to understand Canada's Wind Chill Index.

The Wind Chill Index equates outdoor conditions to an equivalent temperature with no wind. It tells you the degree of chill that your skin senses. By understanding the wind chill index, you can avoid injuries from the cold.

Wind Speed (km/hr)	Temperature (Celsius)									
0	0	-5	-10	-15	-20	-25	-30	-35	-40	-45
10	-3	-9	-15	-21	-27	-33	-39	-45	-51	-57
20	-5	-12	-18	-24	-30	-37	-43	-49	-56	-62
30	-6	-13	-20	-26	-33	-39	-45	-52	-59	-65
40	-7	-14	-21	-27	-34	-41	-48	-54	-61	-68
50	-8	-15	-22	-29	-35	-42	-49	-56	-63	-69
60	-9	-16	-23	30	-36	-43	-50	-57	-64	-71

Source: http://www.almanac.com/content/windchill-chart-canada

When the wind chill goes below -27C, there is a risk of frostbite. What this means is that exposed skin can freeze in 10-30 minutes.

Find out the weather forecast on radio or television, in newspapers or on-line at Environment Canada before dressing to go outside.

Official Languages

Canada has two official languages: English and French. Depending on where you live in Canada, you may need to improve your English or French skills.

Free language training classes are offered across Canada. Your sponsor or settlement counselor will be able to direct you for language testing to determine your language level to see if you require further language training.

Learning another language is always of benefit and classes are offered if you want to improve your language skills or learn another language.

Banking

Financial institutions in Canada are secure. You can feel safe keeping your money in a Canadian bank or credit union.

> **If a Canadian bank exists in your country, you can open a bank account before you arrive.**

Both banks and credit unions offer residential mortgage financing, consumer credit and deposit services, terms deposits, Registered Retirement Savings Plans (RRSPs), Registered Retirement Income Funds (RRIFs), business products, loans, financial counseling, trust and insurance services.

Canada has a national system of banking. This means that no matter where you live in Canada, you can access similar services at the same price at any bank. Shareholders own banks. There are 29 domestic banks, 24 foreign bank subsidiaries and 27 full-service foreign bank branches.[51]

The five major banks in Canada include: Canadian Imperial Bank of Commerce (CIBC), Bank of Montreal (BMO), Bank of Nova Scotia (Scotiabank), Toronto Dominion Bank of Canada (TD) and Royal Bank of Canada (RBC). Other banking institutions also exist in Canada.

Anyone can open a bank or credit union account in Canada, if they provide the required identification. You do not need to have a job or money to deposit to open an account.

Credit unions are owned and controlled by their members. The cost of becoming a member ranges from $5 to $125.

There are approximately 700 different credit unions (caisses populaires in Quebec) in Canada. Credit Unions often offer better value than banks, particularly with competitive and transparent pricing on mortgages.

Bank and credit union debit cards can be used at any ATM across the country 24 hours a day, seven days a week. You can also set up your account to have Internet and/or telephone banking.

Many employers pay their employees through direct deposit. This means you will need a bank or credit union account for your employer to deposit your earnings.

---

[51] Office of the Superintendent of Financial Institutions, May 2014, http://www.osfi-bsif.gc.ca/eng/pages/default.aspx

Currency

Canada uses both coins and paper (polymer) money.

Coins: 5 cents is called a Nickel
10 cents is called a Dime
25 cents is called a Quarter
1 dollar is called a Loonie
2 dollars is called a Toonie

Paper money comes in denominations of $5 (blue), $10 (purple), $20 (green), $50 (red) and $100 (brown).

The one-cent coin was eliminated in Canada. Prices, however, still have one- cent amounts. So, if a price tag says $10.01 or $10.02, you will pay $10.00. If the price tag says $10.03, $10.04, $10.06 or $10.07, you will pay $10.05. If the price tag says $10.08 or $10.09, you will pay $10.10

It will take you some time before you are comfortable knowing what Canadian currency is worth. Try not to convert from your money, i.e., Syrian pound to Canadian dollars. It is best to learn the currency and what it is worth in terms of what it costs to live in Canada and what you can afford to spend.

While you are getting accustomed to the currency, make a monthly budget of your expenditures. Try to stay on budget and not go into debt.

Credit

In Canada, you can apply for one or more credit cards. Credit cards are available from banks and credit unions plus large stores.

Credit means that you borrow money to purchase something now and pay it back later with interest. Interest is the fee that you are charged to borrow the money. Interest rates vary from credit cards to credit card, so it is important to get a credit card with the lowest interest rate possible.

It is extremely important to maintain your credit rating in Canada. Make sure to pay at least the minimum owing each month as shown on your bill. If you can, the best is to pay your bill in full each month.

You need to maintain a good credit rating in order to get loans to purchase large items like a home or car.

Housing

When you come to Canada, you will need housing. Most newcomers initially rent rather than buy. If you are a privately sponsored refugee, your sponsor will help you with rent for your first year in Canada.

There are different types of rental housing or housing you can purchase in Canada. Here is information about the types of rental housing in Canada:

- Rooms – a private bedroom in a large house with shared kitchen and bathroom
- Apartments – A self-contained unit in a building
- Duplexes or triplexes – a house that is divided into two or three units
- Townhouse – Three or more units built side-by-side and share adjoining walls
- Single-family detached – a home that stands alone and sits on its own lot

Tenants have rights and responsibilities and are protected by the law. The tenant is responsible for paying the rent as scheduled, usually once per month. The tenant is responsible for keeping the rental unit clean and well maintained. Multiple families cannot use one apartment unit.

Landlords are the people who own the rental building. The landlord also has rights and responsibilities. The landlord is responsible for keeping the building in good repair and collecting rent. Landlords can raise rent once in a 12-month period. The provincial government determines rent increase amounts. The landlord cannot exceed the legal rental increase.

Typical Canadian Apartment Building

To find a place to rent, first determine the area you want to live in. Ask people about safe neighborhoods to live in. Then, check your local Kijiji website for rentals. Visit several different places before deciding which one to rent. Ask what your rent includes: heat, electricity, parking, water, cable and/or use of a gym or common area.

Once you decide on a place to rent, you will be asked to sign a lease. This is a written contract so be sure to read it before signing. You will also be asked for a security deposit to cover any damage that might happen while you are living in the rental unit. The law requires that your deposit include only the first and last month's rent.

Your housing costs should not exceed 30 – 32% of your gross household income.

Source: Royal Bank of Canada

On the day you move in, check thoroughly and make note or take a photograph of any damage you find, such as carpet holes or stains, scratches on cupboards and/or water stains on ceilings. Ask the landlord to sign the list of damages and keep a copy for your records. You will get your security deposit returned when you vacate if there is no new damage.

When you want to move out of your rental unit, you must give your landlord prior written notice, at least one month or more depending on the province, before the first day of the month when you want to move out. You are also responsible for cleaning your apartment thoroughly once all your possessions are removed.

Many newcomers buy a home after a few years of living in Canada. Again, the first step is to decide what neighborhoods you want to live in and what type of house you can afford.

There are different types of homes you can purchase:

- Condominium – Multi-unit buildings where you purchase a unit
- Semi-detached – Separate land and separate entrances with a common shared wall
- Townhouse – Attached side by side to a series of other homes
- Single Detached – Free-standing house where land and home are owned

Single Family Home in Canada

Meet with a mortgage specialist at your financial institution who can help you determine what you can afford. They will explain that you need a down payment and will tell you the amount of mortgage you qualify for. Once you are pre-approved for a mortgage, then you can determine the size and features of the home you want to purchase. You will need an established, good credit rating to qualify for a mortgage.

Most homebuyers hire a real estate agent to help them purchase a home. Real estates do not cost the purchaser a fee. The home seller pays them. Real estate agents will show you different homes and help you get the best possible purchase price on the home you want to buy. They will assist you in making the official *Offer to Purchase*.

Indoor Temperature Control: Using a Thermostat

You will need to program the thermostat for cooler and warmer months.

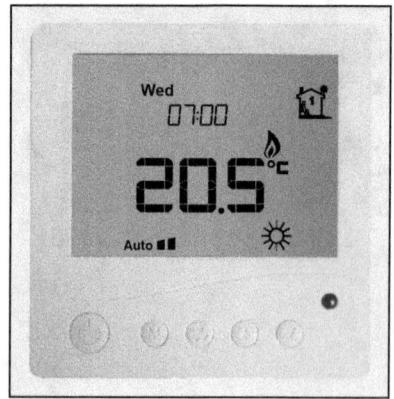

Typically, there are four types of programmable thermostats:

1. 7-day programming that let's you program a different heating/cooling schedule for each day of the week

2. 5-1-1 programming that has one heating/cooling program for the week plus a different heating/cooling program for Saturday and Sunday

3. 5-2 programming that has one heating/cooling program for the week and one heating/cooling program for Saturday and Sunday

4. 1-week programming that has one heating/cooling program for the week that is repeated daily

During the winter months for hours that you are home and awake, it is recommended to set the temperature to 20°C. To save on heating costs, it is common to lower the temperature when you are sleeping or out of the house. Most people lower the temperature to about 16°C.

During the summer months, if you have air conditioning, program the temperature to whatever makes you feel comfortable. When you do not need cooling, manually shut off the air conditioner.

Garbage Collection and Littering

Canadian cities have garbage collection and recycling programs. Garbage is typically collected weekly. In smaller towns and rural areas, there are garbage dumps where you deliver your garbage.

It is illegal in Canada to litter. This means that you cannot throw garbage, waste materials or cigarettes on public or private property. You cannot throw it out of a car window. There are waste and recycling receptacles on major streets and parks.

Recycling is part of garbage collection for your household waste. Typically the following items can be recycled in your Blue Bin:

Plastic
- Plastic bottles and containers #1-7

Paper
- All paper and junk mail
- Milk and juice cartons
- Cardboard boxes
- Paperboard and frozen food boxes
- Newspapers, magazines and catalogues
- Paper bags, paper cups, empty pizza boxes

Glass
- Glass bottles and jars

Metal
- Metal cans, aluminum foil and trays

In some cities, fresh products are also recycled in a Green Bin. Typically the following items can be recycled in your Green Bin:

Food
- Meat, shellfish and fish products
- Dairy products and egg shells
- Coffee grounds, paper filters and tea bags
- Fruit and vegetable scraps
- Candies, cookies and cake
- Baking ingredients and herbs
- Bread, cereal and pasta

Paper
- Paper food packing such as ice cream boxes, flour and sugar bags, used paper towels, napkins and paper plates
- Diapers and sanitary products

Plants and Animal
- Household plants including soil
- Animal waste and cat litter
- Pet food

Check with your local area to see what is specifically accepted in the recycling program where you live.

Education

In Canada, education is a provincial/territorial responsibility and is publicly funded. All provinces require teachers to have a license or certificate to teach in public schools.

Publicly funded schools are free. All boys and girls between the ages of 5 or 6 and 16 or 18 must attend school depending on where you live. This is the law.

Children must go to school every day. If your child is absent due to illness or for personal reasons, you must tell the school.

> **Most Canadian children attend public NOT private schools.**

In Syria there is primary and secondary education levels: 6 years of primary education followed by a 3-year general or vocational training and a 3-year academic or vocational program.

In Canada, there are different education levels based on different grades. The elementary (Kindergarten to Grade 5 or 6) is similar to the primary level in Syria. Secondary level in Canada consists of middle (Grade 6 or 7 to Grade 8 or 9) and high school (Grade 9 or 10 to Grade 12).

From Kindergarten to Grade 12, it is academic education with some optional vocational subjects. However, there are some high schools that offer a full-time vocational programming for high school students. Most vocational programming in Canada occurs at the post-secondary level at a college.

In most schools, boys and girls learn together in the same classroom. There are no school uniforms but most schools have a dress code.

Children attend school Monday to Friday during the school year, except for holidays. Schools operate from September to June and students attend between approximately 9 a.m. to 3:30 p.m.

Summer vacation is during July and August. Winter vacation is between late December to early January. Spring vacation is sometime in March depending on the province.

Publicly Funded High School

Public schools tend to receive better funding and have more programming than privately funded schools.

There are also private and religious schools, which are outside the public funding. Private and religious schools must follow the same curriculum as publicly funded schools. Some private schools are for boys or girls only. There is a fee to send your child to a private or religious school.

> **Private school does not mean better school or better education in Canada.**

There is also home schooling, where children receive their education at home taught by a parent or guardian. Home schooling must follow the same curriculum as publicly funded schools.

Students can attend English-language or French-language schooling. You may also have an option for your children to attend a language immersion school. Immersion programs are offered in many different languages. Check with your local school board to see what languages are offered.

Depending on how close you live to your child's school, your child can walk to school. Children who live too far from the school are bussed. School boards provide buses at minimal to no cost to you. Typically, once your child is 12 years old or in Grade 7, they are expected to take public transportation to school.

Children will get a report card several times during the school year that will tell you about their progress.

> **Parents are encouraged to get involved with the school by meeting your child's teacher, attending parent-teacher meetings, school concerts and plays, and volunteering for events.**

Choosing a Public School

If all teachers are certified and all schools follow the same provincial curriculum, how do you know the best schools for your children?

School choice varies according to city and province. For example, Manitoba parents can select any school in the province provided there are spaces available. In other places, children must attend the local neighborhood school. Consequently, where you select to live may determine where your children attend school.

Ask friends, relatives, acquaintances, mentors and co-workers for their opinions about what schools in your city are considered to be the best.

Differences in Education

Canadian students are under less pressure than students in some other countries.

> ## You may not understand the teaching style used in Canadian classrooms.

In Syria, education tends to be teacher-centered. The teacher talks while the students listen. Classrooms are orderly and the teacher controls the classroom and its activities.

In Canada, education is student-centered. Students and teachers interact equally. Students learn to direct their own learning through participation in group work, by asking questions and by completing tasks independently. The teacher is there to help guide them to self-discovery. Classrooms are often noisy and may appear chaotic.[52]

Canadian teachers use diversified teaching methods including group work, projects, assignments, computer games and role-playing. There is not much, if any, time spent on lectures. Homework assignments are limited. Marks are not based solely on tests and examinations. Class projects, assignment and participation are included in grading students.

Students are expected to participate, use their imagination and creativity, and learn through discovery. You may have to help your child adjust to this new method of teaching and learning. You may have to also adjust as a parent because the system and expectations of teachers and students may be very different from what you are used to.

Canadian Laws

As a permanent resident or citizen of Canada, you are expected to understand and obey Canadian laws.

Unlike in Syria, laws are enforced in Canada.

The police in Canada are not corrupt. They are safe and enforce the law.

---

[52] http://education.cu-portland.edu/blog/classroom-resources/which-is-best-teacher-centered-or-student-centered-education/

> ## Do not offer police officers money, gifts or services in exchange for special treatment.

Offering bribes to anyone working in the legal system is illegal and you can get up to 14 years imprisonment.

You should call the police if you are a victim of a crime, see a crime taking place or know about criminal activities. In Canada, you are presumed innocent until proven guilty.

> ## The emergency police telephone number in all parts of Canada is 911.

Family/Domestic Violence

Family violence is defined as different kinds of abuse that adults or children may have in their families. Domestic violence is not illegal in Syria. Domestic violence is illegal in Canada.

All kinds of physical and sexual abuse, including unwanted sexual activity with your husband or wife, are considered illegal in Canada.

It is a crime to:
- Abuse a child by hitting them with an object, touching them sexually or forcing them into marriage

- Abuse a family member in a financial or psychological way
- Abuse or be cruel to an animal
- Beat, hit, kick or punch a family member including a child or spouse
- Have any sexual contact with a child
- Kill someone including honour killings
- Neglect a child by not providing adequate food, clothing and housing
- Perform female genital circumcision or
- Threaten to hurt someone

Sometimes family violence increases as you go through the cultural adaptation process. Be aware that this tends to happen when the woman in the family becomes employed and is earning money and the man in the family remains unemployed or underemployed.

There are safe shelters for women and children who are abused. Counselling is also available.

> **Discipline of children in some countries is considered abuse in Canada.**
>
> **Victims of family violence should call 911 immediately.**

Disciplining Children

In Syria, physical discipline of children is considered acceptable. In some countries, it is acceptable to slap, hit and/or beat a child as a form of discipline. In Canada, slapping, hitting and/or beating a child with an object may be considered assault. Assault is a criminal offence in Canada.

As a parent, you can use reasonable force to control a child or keep the child safe. This is not considered assault.

Examples of using reasonable force include, "grabbing a child to keep that child from running across a street, carrying a screaming child out of a store or separating two young children who are fighting."[53]

There are legal stipulations on how, and under what conditions, a parent, teacher or caregiver may use reasonable force[54]:

- Use of force is only allowed to help the child learn,
- Correcting behaviour must occur at the time of the circumstance that needs correcting,
- A person must not use force on a child in anger,
- Force can only be used if the child is between two years to twelve years old,
- Reasonable force must be transitory and trifling, which means, for example, a spanking cannot leave a mark on the child that lasts for hours,
- Force cannot be degrading, inhumane or harmful,

---

[53] The Criminal Law and Managing Children's Behaviour, http://canada.justice.gc.ca/eng/rp-pr/cj-jp/fv-vf/mcb-cce/index.html
[54] Ibid

- Person using force must not use an object, i.e., belt, and must not hit or slap the child's head, and

- Force used must be minor, no matter what the child did.

Transportation

All cities and most major towns in Canada have a public system with one or more modes of transportation such as a bus, subway, streetcar or light-rail train. In many cities and towns, there are also transportation services available specifically for people with limited mobility or a disability. You can get more information about public transportation in your city or town by calling a transit information line or visiting the website of your municipal government.

All cities and some towns have one or more companies that offer taxi service. Unlike in many countries, taxis in Canada are expensive. People tend to use them when they have no alternative.

City Bus in Canada

Taxis have automatic meters that use set rates to calculate the cost of your trip. The rates are fixed and cannot be negotiated.

You pay the amount indicated on the meter at the end of the ride. Taxi drivers expect tips particularly if they have loaded your baggage into the trunk (boot) of their vehicle.

To get a taxi, you call the taxi company and they will pick you up at the address you provide. Alternatively, you can catch a taxi at a designated taxi stand such as the ones found at airports. You can try waving your hand at an empty taxi driving by you, but they may or may not stop to collect you.

Most cities have transportation for people with disabilities. It is commonly door-to-door service, which means they pick you up at the address you provide, deliver you to the address you provide and return you to the address you provide.

Bicycles are a common form of transportation in Canada. You do not need a license to ride a bike. You must ride on the road, not the sidewalk, when riding a bike and obey the same rules as car drivers. In many places, it is the law that you must wear a helmet when riding a bicycle. There are exceptions for Sikhs who wear a turban for religious reasons. Some cities have streets with bike lanes, which cars are not allowed to use. If you are riding your bicycle where bike lanes are available, use the bike lanes.

Walking is another form of transportation. There are some laws about walking. For example, you cannot cross the street in the middle of the block. You should cross at a designated crosswalk or at the corner of the street. You must obey traffic lights. Pedestrians have the right of way in Canada. That means that cars must stop for pedestrians at cross walks and at traffic lights. In Canada, always look left first, then right.

Lesbian, Gay, Bi-Sexual, Transgendered, Two Spirit and Queer (LGBTTQ)

Canadians believe and value freedom from discrimination. This may be one of the reasons you are coming to Canada.

In Canada, everyone has the right to live their lives without being discriminated against for race, creed, ethnic background, political beliefs or sexual orientation.

In Syria, homosexuality is against the law and carries a heavy penalty. In Canada, it is socially and legally acceptable to be gay or lesbian (homosexual), bi-sexual, transgendered or two spirit (an Indigenous person who identifies with both male and female gender roles).

Gay and lesbian persons have the same rights and freedoms as all Canadians. They can get married, adopt children, and be on their same-sex spouse's medical and pension plans.

Recreation and Leisure

One of the many benefits of coming to Canada is that you will have more time to spend with your family. Most Canadian provinces have labour laws, which dictate the number of working hours per week. On average, most Canadians work 40 hours per week, 5 days per week.

Every province in Canada has beautiful landscapes for you to enjoy. Visit the many parks, go to the museums, historic sites and lakes, tour the art galleries and participate in activities at recreation facilities.

Enjoying a Summer Day

In Canada, both females and males play sports. During the winter, there is ice hockey, skating, snowboarding and curling plus indoor activities such as swimming, tennis, badminton, volleyball and basketball. During the warmer months, there are sports such as baseball, soccer, swimming and lacrosse. Both children and adults enjoy playing sports.

Children playing Lacrosse

Canada has many lakes, rivers, two oceans and public and private swimming pools. Tragically, hundreds of Canadians die each year in water-related fatalities. Some of these fatalities are newcomers to Canada.

Gimli, Manitoba

Most cities in Canada offer sports and recreational programs. Some recreational activities are subsidized, which means the cost of the program or activity is reasonable.

In some cities, these recreational programs are combined into a booklet called a *Leisure Guide*. You can usually find the *Leisure Guide* or recreational activities under the City's website. This is a good place to start to participate in Canadian recreational activities.

There is also the YMCA, which offers health and fitness, swimming lessons and summer camps for children and youth. For more information, see: **http://ymca.ca/What-We-Offer**

Public swimming pool

It is very important that your children and you learn how to swim.

Swimming lessons are available at most public pools for infants through to adults.

You are never too old to learn how to swim.

CHAPTER 2: COPING WITH CULTURE SHOCK

Stages of Integration

> **All newcomers go through all Stages of Integration**

Different family members go through each stage differently. This can cause friction in the family. For some unknown reason, children and women tend to adapt to the change quicker than men.

Be aware of, and sensitive to your moods and those of others in your family. Post a list of the different stages in a visible place to refer to so you can identify which stages everyone is in.

Here is a brief description of each stage:

Stage 1: Honeymoon

This stage usually occurs the first few days or weeks after arriving in Canada. You may be excited and eager. You feel confident and optimistic. When you arrive, everything is new and exciting. It is like being on a holiday where you are the tourist taking in everything and everyone.

Stage 2: Culture Shock

This stage usually occurs during the first 6 months in Canada. Coping with simple aspects of everyday life become more difficult and challenging.

You start to feel frustrated, disappointed and overwhelmed. You miss your family and friends and feel lonely. This Stage can, for some, last for years.

You start to focus on the differences between yourself and Canada mainly looking at the negative. You may have difficulty sleeping, be sad, homesick and/or exhausted. You may cry unexplainably. You may overeat or not feel like eating at all. You may be angry and lash out at family members. You may feel depressed and start to withdraw.

At this stage, you may dislike Canadian culture and Canadians. You may criticize, mock or show animosity towards Canadians.

Know that this Stage of Integration: Culture Shock is normal and that you will adjust and eventually enjoy living in Canada.

Next you will find a checklist to discover if you may be in the Culture Shock phase of adjustment.

If you check three or more of the symptoms, you might consider getting help through your immigrant settlement agency or an organization that helps newcomers with mental health issues.

Symptoms of Culture Shock Checklist	☑
Feeling lonely	
Feeling sad	
Feeling homesick	
Feeling angry or irritable	
Feeling depressed	
Feeling hopeless	
Can't sleep or sleep too much	
Crying more than normal	
Have bad nightmares	
Have a stomachache	
Don't feel like interacting with others	
Feeling frustrated with new ways of doing things	
Eating too much	
Drinking too much alcohol	
Feeling hostile towards Canadians	
Marital stress and/or family conflict	
When with others from your own culture, complaining about Canada, its systems and blaming Canadians	

Stage 3: Adjustment

You start to become more familiar and comfortable with the culture, people, food and language of Canada. You are less homesick and have started to make friends. You start to get involved in the community and feel more confident and in control. You regain your sense of humour. You now know how to better adapt to living in Canada.

Stage 4: Acceptance

At this stage, you feel comfortable in Canada, have made friends and are involved in the community. You are able to compare both the good and bad of Canada, with the good and bad of your home country. You now know how things are done in Canada. You start to view Canada as your second home.

Stage 5: Integration

At this stage you can now live comfortably in two cultures, your own and Canadian. You adopt certain behaviours from the new culture. You view yourself as a Canadian from (home country) rather than a (home country) living in Canada. You now feel at home.

Post-Traumatic Stress Disorder (PTSD)

Some of you may have left your country due to war or persecution. Leaving your home for these reasons, may cause you to have a delayed response to the trauma or pressures you felt.

Are you having trouble sleeping? Do you have nightmares? Are you feeling lonely and depressed? Are you having an upset stomach or constant headaches?

If you answered yes to any of these questions, you could be suffering from Post-Traumatic Stress Disorder or PTSD. PTSD is a natural reaction to terrible experiences.

It is very important for you to seek professional counseling for PTSD.

As a refugee, you may have witnessed or experienced your friends and family members being tortured or killed. You and your family were forced to leave your home and as such, this would have been a traumatic event that could cause PTSD.

PTSD can affect anyone, including children, long after any real danger has passed. Symptoms can appear months to years after.

There is help in Canada for you, if you are experiencing symptoms of PTSD or depression. Talk to your doctor, your settlement counselor or your sponsor. Contact the Canadian Mental Health Association who can direct you to help: **www.cmha.ca**

If you feel like you are suicidal, call 911 or go to the closest Emergency Department at your local hospital.

If you need someone to talk with immediately, call your local crisis line. You can find crisis telephone lines at: www.partnershformh.ca/resources /find-help/crisi-centres-across-canada/

Working with clients who were attending professional counseling, these things also seemed to help alleviate the depression and sadness.

You can try them to see if any help you feel better:

- Think of what gave you enjoyment and pleasure as a child. For example, maybe you liked soccer or dancing. Try to do that activity at least three times per week. For example, join a soccer team or kick a ball in your yard or at a park. Put on music and dance. Do not worry about who will see you. Just blare the music and dance away some of your stress.

- Find a quiet place in your house where you will not be interrupted. Light a candle and stare at the candle for at least 15 minutes each day. Focus your attention on the flame. If your mind starts to wander, re-focus on the flame.

- Start a daily journal. Each day write three things you are grateful for. They can be small things.

- When you feel more confident, write your story including the traumatic events. Write as if you were writing for a 10-12 year old. This is the most difficult exercise. Once you are finished your story, you have a few options. Gather your family together and burn your story or attach it to a helium balloon and release it into the sky. Self publish the story if you are comfortable and want to keep the story.

> The Symptoms Checklist is not a diagnostic tool. It is only as a guide to indicate when you may need to seek professional care.

Symptoms Checklist

Some Common Symptoms	
Adults	☑
Flashbacks of the traumatic event	☐
Nightmares	☐
Feeling emotionally numb	☐
Feeling strong guilt	☐
Feeling depressed	☐
Feeling excessively worried	☐
Difficulty sleeping	☐
Angry outbursts	☐
Feeling tense	☐
Loss of interest in activities you used to enjoy	☐

Adults cont'd	☑
Fear someone may harm you	☐
Difficulty concentrating	☐
Drug or alcohol abuse	☐
Suicidal thoughts	☐
Pre-School Children	☑
Thumb-sucking or nail-biting	☐
Crying for no apparent reason	☐
Clinging to mother or caregiver	☐
Bedwetting	☐
Fear of dark or sleeping alone	☐
Children	☑
Anxious or depressed	☐
May refuse to go to school	☐
Stomachaches and/or headaches	☐
Re-enact or replay trauma	☐
Sleep disturbances including nightmares	☐
Angry outbursts	☐
Fear of dark	☐

Children cont'd	☑
Unable to concentrate	☐
Teenagers	☑
Risk-taking behaviours	☐
Difficulties in School	☐
Is very self-conscious ⌀	☐
Becomes very rebellious	☐
Becomes withdrawn and depressed	☐
Sleep and eating disturbances	☐
Suicidal thoughts	☐
Drug and alcohol abuse	☐

Sources: HeretoHelp, BC Partners for Mental Health and Addictions Information,
http://www.heretohelp.bc.ca/visions/trauma-and-victimization-vol3/war-trauma-in-refugees,
Caring for Kids New to Canada, Canadian Paediatric Society, http://www.kidsnewtocanada.ca/mental-health/ptsd, eMentalHealth.ca ,
http://m.ementalhealth.ca/index.php?m=article&ID=8885&r=Winnipeg-Regional-Health-Authority, Sirin, Selcuk R. and Rogers-Sirin, Lauren, *The Educational and Mental Health Needs of Syrian Refugee Children*, Migration Policy Institute, October 2015

Remember that there is professional help available in Canada to treat mental health issues such as depression or PTSD. Ask your doctor for help.

CHAPTER 3: SETTLEMENT AND INTEGRATION

Settlement

You have finally arrived in Canada. What do you need to do immediately, in the next few weeks and in the next year?

This section will answer your questions and provide information on adapting successfully and learning how to integrate into Canadian society.

Your First Week

Upon arrival in Canada, there are some things you need to attend to immediately. Buy a street map at a local convenience store to help you navigate. Start exploring. Walk around. Take different bus routes to see where you live.

You MUST apply for a Social Insurance Number (SIN) and a medical insurance health card.

Social Insurance Number (SIN)

Some of you already received your Social Insurance Number when you landed.

A Social Insurance Number (SIN) is a nine-digit number that you require to work in Canada or to receive government benefits. A SIN is issued to one person only. It does not expire and is used throughout your lifetime.

Parents or legal guardians can apply for a SIN on behalf of a minor child. Children who are 12 years of age or older can apply for their own SINs. There is no fee for obtaining a SIN.

For those of you who did not receive a SIN, you must apply for your SIN, in person, at a local Service Canada Centre with original proof of your identity documents. You can find your local Service Canada Centre at: **https://www.canada.ca/en/employment-social-development/corporate/portfolio/service-canada.html or** telephone: **1-800-206-7218**.

When applying for your Social Insurance Number, you must provide an original of one of the following:[55]

- Permanent resident card issued by Immigration, Refugees and Citizenship Canada (IRCC).

- Confirmation of permanent residence issued by IRCC, accompanied by either a travel document (for example, a foreign passport) or alternate photo identification issued by a provincial/territorial authority (for example, a driver's license).

- Record of Landing issued by IRCC before June 28, 2002;

- Verification of Landing issued by IRCC. This document is only acceptable to amend a SIN record or to obtain a confirmation of an existing SIN.

---

[55] http://www.esdc.gc.ca/en/sin/before_applying.page

- Status Verification or Verification of Status issued by IRCC. This document is only acceptable to amend a SIN record or to obtain a confirmation of an existing SIN.

- Additionally, you will need to provide one of the following supporting documents when you apply, if required: Certificate of Marriage, Divorce Certificate, Legal Change-of-Name Certificate, Adoption Order, Request to Amend Record of Landing or a Confirmation of Permanent Residence document. If your application is approved, you will receive your SIN card that day.

Apply for Benefits

If you are a parent, there are a number of federal benefits you may be eligible to receive. You can ask how to apply at the Service Canada Centre when you apply for your SIN or see Family benefits: **https://www.canada.ca/en/services/benefits/family.html**

These benefits include the following:

- Canada Child Benefit (CCB) – Tax-free monthly payment made to eligible families to help with the cost of raising children under the age of 18. Canada Revenue Agency uses information from your income tax and benefit return to calculate how much your CCB payments will be. For more information see: **http://www.cra-arc.gc.ca/bnfts/ccb/menu-eng.html**

- Child Disability Benefit: Tax-free benefit for families who care for a child under age 18 who is eligible for disability tax credit. For more information see: **www.cra-arc.gc.ca/cdb/**

- Family-related Employment Insurance Benefits – For more information on receiving maternity and parental leave, compassionate care benefits as well as special benefits for parents of critically ill children see: **https://www.canada.ca/en/services/benefits/ei /ei-maternity-parental.html**

Some provinces also provide additional benefits. Check the provincial or territorial website for more information on tax benefits to families.

If you are a government-assisted refugee, you will receive financial support from the Canadian government for up to one year from your date of arrival in Canada or until you can support yourself.

If you are a privately sponsored refugee, depending on which program you were sponsored under, your private sponsor will assist you financially for one year. This may or may not be in partnership with the government, which will cover your costs for six months and your private sponsor for the next six months. There are also financial assistance programs for government-assisted refugees and loans for resettled refugees.

If you are a senior, aged 65 and over, you can apply for the Old Age Security (OAS) pension. It is a monthly payment available to seniors who meet the Canadian legal status and residence requirements.

In addition to the OAS pension, there are three types of OAS benefits that you might qualify for:

1. Guaranteed Income Supplement (GIS): If you have a low income, this is a monthly non-taxable benefit that can be added to your OAS pension.

2. Allowance: If you are 60-64 and your spouse or common-law partners is receiving the OAS pension and is eligible for GIS, you might be eligible to receive this benefit.

3. Allowance for the Survivor: If you are 60-64 and widowed, you might be eligible to receive this benefit.[56]

Health Insurance

All Canadian permanent residents can apply for and be covered by government health insurance. You need to apply for a health insurance card as soon as you arrive. The provincial or territorial governments issue health cards.

If you arrived as a refugee, the Canadian government's Interim Federal Health Program (IFHP) provides temporary health-care coverage to those who are not eligible for provincial or territorial health insurance. To apply contact: **http://www.cic.gc.ca/english/refugees/outside/summary-ifhp.asp**

You will need your health insurance card to receive medical care from doctors and at medical clinics and hospitals.

---

[56] https://www.canada.ca/en/services/benefits/publicpensions/cpp/old-age-security.html

British Columbia, Ontario and New Brunswick require permanent residents to wait a certain period (up to three months) before receiving government health insurance. All other provinces provide healthcare coverage immediately.

If you plan to travel outside Canada, you must buy private travel insurance from an insurance company.

Medical Emergencies

There are different types of medical emergencies. For life threatening or other serious conditions, call 911 for an ambulance. The ambulance will quickly transport the patient to the hospital. There is a charge for the ambulance service, which differs in each province. Most workplaces offer extended health benefits that cover ambulance fees.

For other emergencies such as a broken bone, you are expected to transport the patient to the Emergency Room at your nearest local hospital.

For non-emergencies such as a sinus infection or sore throat, you can either make an appointment with your family doctor or attend a Walk-In Clinic. Walk-In Clinics are typically open 7 days a week and have different doctors on call to take non-emergency patients.

Register Your Children in School

Upon arrival, you MUST register your school-age children in elementary, middle or high school.

Visit your nearest local school or school board to register your child. When you register your child, you will need to bring: Permanent Resident Card, Record of Landing or Confirmation of Permanent Residence, your child's birth certificate and your child's vaccination certificate if available. If you do not have your child's birth certificate or vaccination certificate, you must still register your children in school. You will need to show some identification with your current address in Canada.

If you have records from your child's previous schools that are translated into English or French, bring them with you to the school when registering your child.

The school may assess your child to determine what grade they should be placed in and whether they need additional support. Many schools have settlement workers who can speak your language and can assist in answering your questions.

Buy Food and Household Goods

Most communities have one or more large supermarkets that sell all kinds of food and groceries. Some of the larger grocery store names include: Costco, IGA, Loblaw's, Safeway, Sobeys, The Real Canadian Superstore, No Frills, Saveonfoods and Wal-Mart.

Typical large Canadian grocery store

In most cities in Canada, you will be able to find food from your home country. Many items are sold in the large supermarkets and at local ethnic grocery stores.

Unlike in Syria where you bargain and barter when buying something, in Canada, you do not bargain or barter for a lower price. All prices are set and displayed for each item. You will pay a provincial sales tax (PST) and a 5% federal sales tax (GST) on many goods and services. New Brunswick, Nova Scotia, Newfoundland and Labrador, Ontario and Prince Edward Island have harmonized their provincial sales tax with GST. This is called HST.

There are shopping malls, which have a variety of different stores selling household goods, clothing and personal items. There are also second-hand and consignment stores that sell used clothing, furniture and other household items.

People also sell things they no longer need. You can find items online at **www.kijiji.ca** or at yard or garage sales (held at people's private homes usually on Saturday mornings during the nicer weather). You can negotiate/bargain for second-hand items sold online or at yard sales.

When you first arrive in Canada, second-hand shops, purchasing items online and buying a second-hand car are more cost effective than buying new.

In the summer months, you can find fresh vegetables and fruits at local farmer's market.

Banking

Shortly after you arrive, go to your local bank or credit union to open a bank account. You will need to show your landed immigrant papers and any other identification you have to prove your residency.

Buy a Cell Phone (Mobile)

It is a smart idea to purchase a cell phone and mobile network plan shortly after you arrive. The three largest service providers in Canada are Rogers Wireless, Bell Mobility and TELUS. A cell phone will allow you to contact different service organizations and look for a job.

Immigrant Settlement Services

Canada wants and needs immigrants. To help you get a good start, the Government of Canada funds immigrant/refugee-serving agencies in each province.

Immigrant-serving organizations assist newcomers settle, obtain language training, find work, get a mentor and integrate. There are no fees for these services. Most provide services to Permanent Residents for their first three years in Canada.

You can find your local settlement agency at:
http://www.cic.gc.ca/english/newcomers/map/service s.asp

For agencies that specifically serve refugees:
http://ccrweb.ca/en/members#zoom=3&lat=52.26816 &lon=-96.50391&layers=TB

Your First Few Weeks

Take a Tour of Where You Live

Many cities offer half or full-day sightseeing tours. A sightseeing tour will provide you with information about the city. It will give you a sense of what different parts of the city look like. You can ask questions about different locations.

> **Before you decide what neighbourhood you want to live in, it is a good idea to spend some time discovering the place where you have located.**

Another way to find out about different neighborhoods is to take different bus routes to explore what each is like. You can either stay on the bus or get off and walk around. For those of you who live in a town or rural area, walk around and see the sites.

If you have the time, volunteer for Meals on Wheels, a charitable organization that delivers midday meals to the elderly. You can be a driver or a food deliverer. You can commit to one route or be a spare and be called when no one else is available to go on different routes. It is a great way to learn about where you live, while at the same time meeting some different people.

Find Medical Care

According to the World Health Organization, for those of you who have been in refugee camps, the main health concerns are upper respiratory tract infections, diarrhea and skin conditions. You may also have chronic diseases such as gastro-intestinal complaints, intestinal parasites, hypertension, asthma, diabetes and/and cardiovascular conditions.[57]

As part of your medical screening to be accepted to Canada, doctors will have assessed your medical condition and you may have received treatment. It will be very important for you to follow-up with your own family doctor.

Within a short time after your arrival, you will need to find a family doctor and dentist. How do you find a family doctor, dentist or optometrist? Most cities and provinces have a website or telephone number, which you can call to find the names of doctors in your area that are accepting new patients.

Make an appointment to see your new family doctor. You can do this by telephoning the doctor's receptionist. Take all your available medical records with you to the appointment.

To find a dentist or an optometrist in Canada, look in the telephone Yellow Pages or online. Ask your family or friends for names of dentists that they know. Then, call to see if the dentist is accepting new patients.

---

[57] World Health Organization, http://www.emro.who.int/jor/jordan-news/syrian-refugees.html

Dentists are not free in Canada. Different dentists charge different rates, usually based on how long they have been in practice. Many employers offer health benefits that cover a portion of dental charges.

Purchasing Medicine

The Federal Government of Canada regulates prescription drugs. Provincial health insurance does not cover the total cost of prescription drugs.

Canadians and Permanents Residents are responsible for the cost of prescription drugs provided to them outside hospitals and nursing homes. Some employers offer insurance coverage for prescription drugs provided through supplementary health plans.

Each provincial and territorial government offers a drug benefit plan for eligible groups. For more information to see what your province or territory offers see: **http://www.hc-sc.gc.ca/hcs-sss/pharma/acces/ptprog-eng.php**

There are two types of medication available in Canada: over-the-counter and prescription. Over-the-counter medications are used to prevent or treat injuries or conditions that individuals can recognize and manage on their own behalf. Over-the-counter drugs would include such medicine as aspirin, ibuprofen, cough syrup, throat lozenges and eye drops.

In some areas of the world, medicine can be purchased directly at a pharmacy without a prescription from a doctor. This is very different in Canada.

Health Canada regulates and approves pharmaceutical drugs (medicine that requires a doctor's prescription in order to purchase). This ensures the safety and quality of drugs provided to patients.

For most illnesses that require medications that patients cannot manage on their own, seek medical attention from a physician to obtain a prescription. In some provinces, pharmacists are allowed to provide vaccinations and some prescription medications.

Find a More Permanent Home

By now, you have checked out different neighborhoods and have narrowed down your search of where you want to live. You must decide if you rent or purchase. Most newcomers decide to rent and wait a few years until they purchase a home.

You need to determine a budget of what you can afford to pay monthly.

Here are some of the costs to consider:
- Rent
- Tenant or Home Owner Insurance
- Utilities
  - Heat
  - Water
  - Electricity
  - Telephone
  - Internet service
  - Cable for television

Start going to see different rental apartments:

- Ask questions about what is included in the rent.
- Ask what types of people live in the apartment?
- Are there families or mainly seniors or single people?
- What schools are nearby?
- What bus, subway or light-rail train routes are nearby?
- Are there grocery stores nearby?
- What is the maximum number of people that can live in the apartment?

For low-income families, there are subsidies available to help you pay your rent. For more information about subsidies, see: **https://www.cmhc-schl.gc.ca/en/co/prfinas/**

When you decide on a place to rent, here is a checklist for you to use.

Rental Checklist

Checklist	☑
Read, understood and signed written tenancy agreement	
Checked rental unit for damage and recorded/photographed	
Got landlord to sign the list of damages and kept copy	
Arranged for utilities not provided by landlord: electricity, water, heat, cable for television, telephone and internet service	
Bought tenants or home owner's insurance	

Buy a Computer or Laptop

Purchasing a computer or laptop and Internet service should be another priority as most jobs advertised in Canada accept applications on-line. You will be able to search for jobs, write your cover letters and resumes, and submit your applications if you have a computer with Internet access. Public libraries also have computers that you can use until you are able to afford your own computer.

If you do not know how to use a computer, there are usually local social service agencies that provide free or low cost computer lessons. Ask your counselor at the local immigrant-serving agency where you can take free computer lessons.

Credential Recognition for Regulated Professions

Each province regulates certain professions. If you worked in what is a regulated profession in Canada, you may be able to get re-certified to work in that profession in Canada.

Visit your profession's regulatory body to begin or continue the process of getting licensed in your profession or trade.

If you are asked to take a specific English course for your profession, attend more courses at college, university and/or your professional organization, participate in a Bridging Training Program or obtain clinical or workplace experience before you are allowed to write your licensing exam, consider the cost and time of participating.

Weigh the pros and cons. Can you afford to do this when you first arrive? Should you consider an alternative career or a new profession? If you can afford the time and money it costs, you should strongly pursue your licensure.

Your First Year

Find Childcare

There can be challenges finding childcare in Canada. Some have very long wait lists.

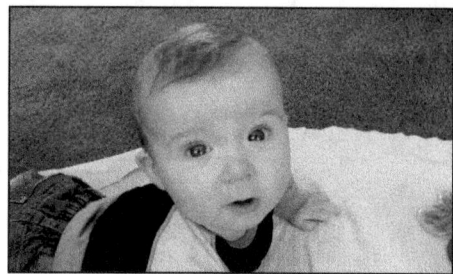

Find Childcare

According to the law, children under the age of 12 cannot be left at home alone in Canada. Once you are working, you will need daycare for your young children.

There are several different options for childcare in Canada: licensed daycares, nursery schools, home-based daycares and school based before-and-after school programs. Each will charge a daily fee to provide services. Many have long waiting lists, so put your child on a wait list even when you are unemployed, as you may be employed by the time the child is accepted.

Get a Driver's License

You need a driver's license to drive in Canada. It is illegal to drive without a license. Driver's licenses are issued by the province or territory where you live. In most provinces, you must be 16 years of age to legally drive. You must carry your driver's license with you at all times when you are driving. Both men and women drive in Canada.

If you have a valid driver's license from your country or an international driver's license, you may be able to drive for a short time period after you arrive. Contact your local provincial government driver-licensing department to enquire.

The process for getting a driver's licence varies across provinces and territories. You may have to write a written exam on the rules of the road and then take a driving test.

If you are a new driver, it is important to take driving lessons from a professional driving school. You can practice driving with a licensed driver who is a family member or friend before taking the road test.

If you are an experienced driver, it is a good idea to pay a professional driving school for a couple of lessens to refresh you on the driving rules in Canada and parallel parking.

Once you have your driver's license, it is valid for a period of time before you have to pay for its renewal. It is also valid across Canada and the United States. If you move permanently to another province, then you must obtain a driver's license from that province.

Purchase Car Insurance

There are different options for car insurance depending on the province where you live.

In some provinces, car insurance is available through private insurance companies. Ontario has the highest private auto insurance rates in Canada. Alberta is the second most costly.

Driver's insurance rates are determined by actual risk factors. For example, a younger, inexperienced driver would pay a higher rate.

In provinces with private car insurance, it is important to get quotes from different insurers prior to making a decision about which one to buy.

It is strictly illegal to drive without car insurance in Canada.

Public car insurance, such as in Saskatchewan and Manitoba, coverage is provided by the provincial government. It can be purchased through any local insurance dealer. Standard rates apply to every driver, regardless of age or gender.

Traffic Laws

Driving laws are strictly enforced in Canada, and penalties for breaking the law are generally costly.

There are too many laws to list fully here, so you will need to learn and understand Canadian traffic laws. The two most important to know are that you must have a driver's license to drive and you must be covered by car insurance to drive.

If the police stop you for breaking a traffic law, STAY in your car.

The police officer will come to your car to talk to you. You will be asked to provide your driver's license and automobile registration.

Do NOT try to drive away.

Drinking And Driving

The legal age to drink alcohol in Canada differs from province to province. The legal age in British Columbia, Saskatchewan, Ontario, New Brunswick, Prince Edward Island, Nova Scotia, Northwest Territories, Nunavut and Yukon is 19 years of age. The legal age in Alberta, Manitoba and Quebec is 18 years of age.

Most provinces have very strict laws about driving after you have been drinking alcohol. If the police stop you after you have been drinking alcohol, you could have your vehicle taken away, lose your driver's license, pay fines, and possibly go to jail.

Parking Tickets

If you park in a no parking area or if you do not put enough money in a parking meter, you may have to pay a fine. Be sure to check the signs on the street that will tell you, if and when, you can park on that street. You cannot park in front of a fire hydrant (which fire fighters use to get water to a fire), or at places where public buses stop to pick up passengers.

Seat Belts and Child Safety Seats

Seat belts are mandatory to wear for all passengers and drivers in every province in Canada. Fines for not wearing seatbelts can be costly.

Child car seat legislation is different in each province, so it is important to know and understand the law. If you have an infant, child or children that require car seats, buy approved age appropriate car seats that meet the Canada Motor Vehicle Safety Standards. Ask how to properly install the car seat into a vehicle.

Speeding

In most cities in Canada, the speed limit is 50 kilometres per hour (km/h) unless otherwise posted. Outside the city, the speed limit is higher usually between 90 – 110 km/hr. In some places, the speed limit is reduced to 30 km/hour near schools. Fines for driving faster than the speed limit can be very expensive.

Texting and Hands Free Talking

It is against the law to text or use a handheld device such as a cell phone (mobile) while driving. Many cars come equipped with Bluetooth, which enables you to make and receive phone calls hands free.

Attend College or University

One way to improve your competiveness is to study in Canada. You can take a whole new career path or you can take a few courses that compliment your foreign education.

Many newcomers think that if they take more education, they will be more employable. This is not necessarily true.

Educational qualifications are only assessed during the screening process for the job interview. Most employers are looking for more than just education. They want you to have the soft skills necessary to work in the Canadian workplace. Sometimes, volunteering, doing an internship or working in a related career will be more important than a list of educational qualifications.

> **Canadian employers may not recognize your foreign education because they do not understand how it equates to Canadian education.**

In Canada, there are different types of post-secondary education and institutions. You want to select an institution that is "recognized". "Recognized" means that the provincial or territorial government has granted the authority to that institution to grant degrees, diplomas, and certificates.

To be accepted into university or college you must meet the admission requirements established by each educational institution.

Each university and college determines its own admission requirements for each program. Each university and college assesses foreign education for admissions along with language skills. You must have the appropriate language level to qualify for the academic program.

College

Colleges offer degree, diploma and certificate programs that you pay tuition to attend.

College programs are typically under 3 years in length. Many include a work co-op experience where you gain practical work experience, learn about the Canadian workplace culture and get work references. Generally speaking, College tuition is about half the cost of university tuition.

Most College programs are work oriented.

For more information about Colleges across Canada, see Member Directory: **https://www.collegesinstitutes.ca/our-members/member-directory/**

> ## Both university and college graduates are highly respected in Canada.

University

Universities offer degree programs that you pay tuition to attend. There are three levels of degrees: Bachelors, Master's and Doctorate.

Undergraduate degree programs where you obtain a Bachelor's degree are typically 3-4 years in length.

University programs tend to be more academic focused.

For more information about Universities across Canada, see: **http://www.univcan.ca/universities/member-universities/**

Joint/Collaborative College and University Programs

Many Colleges and Universities across Canada have partnered to offer a combination of applied education (an approach to learning focusing on subjects that apply to the real world) with theoretical learning.

Students enrolled in Joint Programs graduate with a university degree as well as a college diploma. In some cases, it is a less expensive way to obtain a university degree, as during the College component of the program the tuition is usually less than the tuition for the same University components. For more information on Joint Programs see:
http://www.univcan.ca/universities/universities-and-colleges-partners-in-education/

Settlement Checklist

	To Do	☑
1	Apply for Social Insurance Number	
2	Apply for Health Insurance Card	
3	Register Children in School	
4	Set up a Bank or Credit Union Account	
5	Apply for Government Benefits	
6	Buy a Cell Phone and Cell Phone Plan	
7	Visit local Immigrant-Serving Agency	
8	Take a Tour of Where You Live	
9	Find a Doctor and Dentist	
10	Find a more Permanent Home	
11	Buy a Computer or Laptop with Internet Access	
13	Find Childcare	
14	Get Driver's License and Car Insurance	
15	Improve English or French Language Skills	
16	Participate in community activities	
17	Get help if you need it	
18	Be patient and Do Not Give Up	

CHAPTER 4: FIND A JOB

Preparing to Find a Job

In your home country, you knew how to find a job or set up a business. Canada is a different country and you will need to learn different job search strategies.

Your local settlement agency may teach job search skills and/or deliver programs to connect you with potential employers.

Most jobs in the Canada are in what is called the "hidden job market". This means that most jobs in Canada are found through your network.

When preparing to find a job in Canada, you will need to know how to write a custom cover letter and resume that is tailored to the job advertisement. You will need to know about Canadian job interviews and how to answer interview questions. You will need to be able to show how your past work experience outside Canada is transferable to the Canadian workplace. Once you are hired you will need to know about the Canadian workplace culture and how to behave appropriately in your workplace.

You will also need to determine if your occupation is a regulated or non-regulated occupation in the province you are living in. If you are in a regulated profession or trade, you must obtain certification before you can practice your profession. Some professions are regulated in some provinces and not in others. If you are in a non-regulated profession, you can apply for jobs immediately.

The Government of Canada's Job Bank provides information about skill requirements and job opportunities based on your occupation and location: **www.jobbank.gc.ca**

Understand the Labour Market

Labour market information can help job seekers understand where job opportunities exist across the country.

Labour market information provides data about what jobs and skills employers are looking for, and which industries are hiring. It also provides information on what job trends are for the future.

For current information on job market trends see:
https://www.jobbank.gc.ca/LMI_bulletin.do

For Canadian occupational projections see:
http://occupations.esdc.gc.ca/sppc-cops/w.2lc.4m.2@-eng.jsp

Get a License to Practice Your Profession

Each profession and trade has different certification requirements depending on the province. You cannot practice or work in your profession without a license if it is a regulated occupation.

Step 1: Determine if your profession is regulated in the province you reside in. Commonly regulated professions include ones where the public's safety is concerned including healthcare, financial and legal services, engineering and most skilled trades.

Step 2: Determine what regulatory organization is responsible for providing you with an assessment of your qualifications and certification.

Step 3: Contact the regulatory organization to see what procedures and documents are required to become licensed. If you do not have documents, ask the regulatory organization if they can still assess you. The Canadian Information Centre for International Credentials (**www.cicic.ca**) has information about licensing and regulatory bodies across Canada.

The licensing process typically has three components:
1. Assessment of your educational documents
2. Assessment of your work experience
3. Writing the licensing exam

Depending on the results of the assessments, you may be asked to upgrade or attend a Bridging Program or you may be eligible to write the exam directly.

Bridging Programs are designed to give internationally educated professionals training and experience to fill the gaps to prepare for licensing and working in a Canadian workplace. They are typically offered through joint programs between the regulatory body and a university or college.

Getting licensed can be costly and take a long time. While you are in the process of licensing, you should determine your transferable skills and consider alternative careers.

Loans for Internationally Trained Immigrants

Immigrant Access Fund Canada provides loans of up to $10,000 to internationally trained immigrants and refugees. The purpose of the loan is to assist internationally trained immigrants obtain Canadian licensing and/or training to be able to practice in their professional field.

For more information, see: **http://www.iafcanada.org**

Transferable Skills

Transferable skills are employment skills that you can take with you from one job to another. For example, analytical, communication, computer, creativity, leadership, listening, numeracy, organizational, problem-solving, supervisory, teamwork and time management skills are all transferable skills. No matter what profession or trade you are in, these skills are important to all employers.

Transferable skills may also be referred to as the soft skills you bring to the workplace. Employers look for employees who can demonstrate suitable transferable skills. It is important for you to identify and be able to provide examples of your transferable skills.

How can you identify your transferable skills?

Start by analyzing each of the jobs you have held, to identify what skills you used doing those jobs. These are the transferable skills that will become part of your resume and can be used to answer job interview questions.

When looking for a job in Canada, you may not have direct experience working in a particular area, but you will be able to describe to a prospective employer how the skills you have acquired throughout your career are transferable to the new job.

During job interviews, hiring managers often ask more questions about your soft skills or your transferable skills than your technical skills. Interviewers expect you to provide concrete examples of your transferable skills to show the employer that you are a "good fit" for the position.

Use the Transferable Skills Inventory to identify your transferable skills along with examples.

Transferable Skills Inventory

Transferable Skills	Able to:	☑	Examples:
Accept and Provide Constructive Criticism	Offer and receive valid and well-reasoned positive and negative opinions about the work of others in a friendly manner		
Analytical and Problem Solving	Assess a situation, gather relevant information and solve both complex and uncomplicated problems and concepts		
Communication	Express yourself clearly in both verbal and written form		

Transferable Skills	Able to:	☑	Examples:
Conflict Resolution	Reach a mutually acceptable agreement when there is a disagreement or dispute		
Continuous Learning	Continue to always develop and improve your knowledge and skills		
Creativity	Solve problems through new and innovative methods		
Flexible	Adapt to change without resistance		

Transferable Skills	Able to:	☑	Examples:
Human Relations	Use interpersonal skills for resolving conflict, relating to and helping people		
Initiative	Readiness and ability to take action and follow through with a plan, project or task		
Intercultural	Demonstrate understanding of other cultures and skills to interact in a cross-culturally sensitive manner		

Transferable Skills	Able to:	☑	Examples:
Internet and Social Media	Understand how to use computer, word processing, internet, email, spreadsheets, presentation software		
Interpersonal	Communicate effectively with colleagues, clients and various stakeholders		
Leadership	Influence and inspire others in support of a common goal		
Listening	Listen attentively and clearly articulate the purpose and content of a conversation		

Transferable Skills	Able to:	☑	Examples:
Local Language Skills	Communicate verbally and in written form using local jargon and idioms used in your area and in your particular industry		
Management	Supervise, direct and guide staff in the successful completion of tasks and goals		
Organization	Use your time, energy and resources in an effective manner		
Planning	Conceptualize future needs and solutions for meeting those needs		

Transferable Skills	Able to:	☑	Examples:
Presentation Skills	Present in a confident and clear manner to small and large groups		
Small Talk	Chat about common and local topics such as weather, sports, restaurants, movies		
Teamwork	Collaborate with others to achieve a desired result		
Time Management	Set priorities and meet deadlines		

Alternative Career

Becoming licensed in your profession in Canada can be a long, costly and challenging process. Many internationally educated professionals need to complete some form of skills upgrading or education before they can write their licensing exam.

As a result, you might consider pursuing an alternative career where you can transfer your current skills, knowledge, education, and work experience to another profession. Some individuals choose an alternative career as a permanent choice. Others choose a related career while pursuing licensing of their profession. The decision is up to you.

Following are some examples of professions and alternative or related careers.

Profession	Alternative Career
Construction Worker	• Cabinetmaker • Grounds Maintenance • Woodworker
Engineer	• Supply Chain Management • Technician or Technologist • Technical Consultant or Sales
Medical Laboratory Technologist	• Health Information Technologist • Pathologist Assistant • Technical Sales Specialist
Nurse	• Healthcare Aide • Healthcare Educator • Medical Sales Representative

Profession	• Alternative Career
Teacher	• Corporate Trainer
	• Academic Advisor
	• Sales Representative
Social Worker	• Community Worker
	• Counselor
	• Settlement Worker

Find a Job

Like most newcomers to Canada, you will face many barriers in finding employment at your skill level. Once employed, you will also face many implicit and overt barriers. Some managers and colleagues may not be familiar with your cultural behaviours. You will have challenges understanding some of their expressions and their expectations of soft skills.

As with many newcomers, you will also feel pressure to find a job as soon as possible to fulfill financial commitments and to feel like you have re-established yourself professionally in Canada.

Take advantage of all the settlement services and programs provided where you live.

If you do not have adequate English or French language skills, attend language classes.

> **To be successful in the Canadian workplace, one must be able to communicate effectively.**
>
> **Take the opportunity and time to acquire appropriate language skills.**

There are several things you may need to have, before you can obtain a good job in your field:

- Communication skills at the appropriate level to work successfully in your profession

- Accreditation of your profession, if regulated

- A professional network

- Soft skills and possibly Canadian work experience

- Skills to write a Canadian-style resume and cover letter

- Skills on how to answer Canadian-style interview questions

- Knowledge and understanding of Canadian workplace culture

When you begin your job search, you will need a Canadian-style cover letter and resume. You must also be prepared for a Canadian-style interview.

Do research to find companies and organizations that hire people in your field.

Visit job search websites such as:

- **www.jobbank.gc.ca**
- **www.indeed.ca**
- **www.wowjobs.ca**
- **www.workopolis.com**

Build your Network

There is a common expression in Canada, "It's not what you know, it's who you know." When it comes to finding a job, who you know becomes very important.

Networking is, and should be, part of your career planning and development.

As a newcomer, you may only know a few people in Canada. You will have to actively work to build and develop your personal and professional network.

A network is that group of people whom you interact with regularly – your family, friends, friends of friends, neighbours, teachers, faith community, co-workers and bosses. Networking occurs every time you participate in a community event such as when you volunteer, when you attend a school event, when you attend a child's activity or talk to a neighbor.

Most people in Canada learn about job openings through their network. Turning your personal network into a professional network means talking about your goals, your interests, your strengths, your skills and how you can contribute to a professional environment.

Networking is a skill that can help you find a job, get a promotion and become close with leaders in your industry.

Networking is about building connections and long-term relationships with professional contacts. Networking is an effective strategy to help uncover hidden job opportunities.

> **In Canada, 80% of all jobs are never advertised. This is called the "hidden" job market.**

The benefits of networking for you are:

- Building relationships
- Increasing opportunities
- Raising profile
- Gaining advice and support
- Generating referrals
- Making new friends

Learning how to network effectively is one of the most powerful tools an individual can use to advance their personal and professional life. But if you have never done it before, it can be intimidating.

How to Become a Successful Networker

What to Do		☑
Prepare Ahead:		
1	**Identify Your Strengths**	• Develop a list of your talents, strengths and skills sets	
2	**Identify People**	• Identify people you already know • Identify where you can meet new people, i.e., ethnic associations, language classes, community centres, gyms, volunteer placements, mentorship placements, informational meetings, LinkedIn, Twitter • Identify professional network opportunities, i.e., conferences	
3	**Research**	• Research the company, industry or career of your contacts.	
4	**Plan what you want to say**	• Identify how you can help people now and in the future • Develop some questions to ask about your contact's areas of expertise • Prepare a 1-2 minute introductory script highlighting your name, background, skills and accomplishments (often referred to as an Elevator Pitch) • Avoid asking for a job	

5	**Dedicate Time for Networking**	• Set goals for yourself of how many networking contacts you will connect with each week • Identify attendees and who you would like to talk with	
6	**Be Visible**	• Focus on meeting new people • Engage people in conversation • Ask for information and advice, not a job • Try to find common interests • Ask for introductions and referrals	
7	**How to Finish**	• Towards the end of any conversation, ask how you can be of help • Exchange business cards (make one for yourself if you are not employed) • Thank them for the conversation and tell them you are looking forward to keeping in contact	

Follow-Up and Follow Through

8	**Stay Connected**	• Keep in touch with your new contacts • Send a thank you email or card to your new contact for any help, referrals or resources s/he shared	
9	**Stay Active**	• Stay active on social media with your contacts and prospective contacts • If you made a commitment to help, follow through with your promise	

Develop Your Elevator Pitch

An elevator pitch is a very brief summary about you and your value to a prospective employer. The name "elevator pitch" reflects the idea that it is possible to deliver a summary about you in the time it takes to ride an elevator – approximately 30 seconds.

You should be prepared to attract interest, capture your audience's attention quickly, and highlight what makes you unique. You use your elevator pitch when networking and in job interviews.

When preparing your elevator pitch, here are some questions to think about:

- What do you do well? Think in terms of your accomplishments and 2-3 of your best transferable skills.

- What is your greatest strength? This can be a skill set you are aware of, or one where you have received praise.

- What is your goal? This is not just your personal goal to get a job but includes how you can help an employer solve a problem. Your goal becomes the employer's solution.

- What is your motivation? For example, this can be that you enjoy doing the work that you do. It can be because you want to help others benefit from your work.

Here are the steps to deliver your elevator pitch:

About You
- Smile.

- Greeting and Introduction (shake hands): Name and profession.

What You Have to Offer

- Emphasize concrete accomplishments and skills. Select accomplishments and skills that would be of the most interest to your listener.

- Highlight your uniqueness: Think about what really sets your work and experience apart from others in your industry.

What are the Advantages

- State what you can do for them.

Be prepared to answer questions. Let the listener hear the commitment in your voice and your words. Make direct eye contact.

Keep it short. Refine your elevator pitch as your professional life continues to grow and change.

Gain Canadian Work Experience

Many Canadian employers are unsure whether you will be a "good fit" in their organization. A "good fit" means you have the required technical and soft skills, experience, work ethic and personality of those currently working in the organization.

The employer may wonder if you have sufficient language and communication skills, and are knowledgeable about Canadian workplace standards, technologies and culture. Employers may eliminate you from the selection and hiring process because of their concerns about your lack of soft skills, which are gained through Canadian work experience.

There are several ways to gain Canadian work experience:
- Volunteer
- Job shadow
- Internship
- Temporary work

Note that it is illegal in the Province of Ontario to require Canadian work experience.

Volunteer

Volunteering is where you work for no salary. It is very common and highly valued in Canada. Most Canadians volunteer throughout their lifetime and career.

For you as a newcomer to Canada, volunteering offers many benefits:
- You will significantly improve your communication skills and knowledge of soft skills
- You will learn business etiquette
- Make new friends
- Build your network
- Gain practical work experience and Canadian job references.

You can find volunteer opportunities at:
http://volunteer.ca/volunteer-centres

Job Shadow

Job Shadowing is where you ask people in your professional network if you can spend some time in their company learning about the different jobs related to your field. You follow someone around for a day. You will learn about the workplace culture, business communications and small talk, and may gain Canadian job references.

Internships

Internships are where you work for an employer and the government subsidizes your salary. Internships are not offered for all professions. You can enroll in internships through your local settlement agency. There may be wait lists, so put your name in as quickly as possible on the wait list.

Mentorship

A mentor is someone who guides others to help them achieve their personal and/or career goals. The role can be informal or formal. They can be a counselor, a trusted resource, a coach, a role model, a senior manager or someone who provides emotional support.

Typically, mentors share knowledge, provide guidance and advice on careers, resources, workplace culture and networking opportunities, and offer encouragement to the mentee. Mentors help you feel comfortable with self-promotion, a Canadian tactic for getting noticed and getting a job.

> **A mentor can play a strong role in easing your transition into the Canadian workplace.**

When you are employed, ask your manager if the organization has a mentor program or if someone could be your mentor. Ask that mentor to help you understand how to interpret the Canadian workplace culture, the organizational culture and what the expectation of being a "good employee" in that company entails.

Ask the mentor to help you understand the rules and customs of your new environment - what are the expectations of teamwork, expectations of managers, constructive feedback, how to engage in small talk, concepts of time and punctuality, how to resolve workplace conflict, workplace etiquette and what equality in the workplace actually means.

Canadian-style Cover Letters

A cover letter is your sales pitch to the employer. It tells the employer why they should contact you for an interview, and why you are the best fit for the job. Your cover letter is your first opportunity to impress an employer. It should compel the employer to want to read your resume.

Cover letters identify the job you are applying for, and provide additional information about your skills and experiences that are not highlighted in your resume.

> **Your cover letter must capture the attention of the Hiring Manager.**
>
> **Cover letters should detail EVERY requirement stated in the job advertisement**

When writing your cover letter, the first step is to analyze the job advertisement and determine the most important skills the employer is looking for.

The next step is to address how you will meet the employer's needs.

The first sentence of your cover letter should emphasize the major selling points and skills that you would bring to the job.

The body of the letter is used to demonstrate that you can perform the duties listed in the job advertisement. Think about what you have accomplished in your past jobs and which are transferable skills, experience and attributes to the new job. Emphasize this in the body of the letter and include results in your cover letter.

Conclude your cover letter with a powerful statement about discussing your skills, experience and achievements in more detail at an interview.

Your cover letter must be easy to read. Use Arial 11 pt. font or Time New Roman 12 pt. font with normal margins. A cover letter is 1-2 pages maximum in length. It should contain no spelling or grammatical errors.

Most settlement agencies will help you prepare a basic cover letter or you can hire someone to write your cover letter for you.

Sample cover letters can be found in Appendix 1.

Canadian-style Resumes (CV)

When you are applying for jobs in Canada, you will be expected to submit a resume with your cover letter. Your resume has to be Canadian-style and customized to the job you are applying for.

What is a Canadian-style resume?

It is a summary of your work experience and education highlighting your major accomplishments. It is maximum 2 pages in length and is written in Arial 11 pt. font or Times New Roman 12 pt. font with normal margin sizes.

Canadian-style resumes do not contain a photo or personal information such as gender, age, marital status, father's name or religion. They do not contain school grades.

Canadian-style resumes contain action verbs to describe each talent, strength and accomplishment. Action verbs can be found on the Internet.

Most settlement agencies will help you prepare a basic resume listing your different employers and responsibilities. However, you should be aware that the resume will not be customized to each job advertisement, and it is unlikely to describe your accomplishments. You will be expected to do this on your own.

Remember that you will be competing with Canadian-born applicants who know how to write a customized cover letter and resume. You want your resume to be noticed amongst the hundreds of applications that employers receive for each job advertised.

The most important thing to remember when writing a resume is to customize it to the job advertisement. Ensure that you address all *must have* and *desired* requirements. Include your accomplishments not your job responsibilities. Make sure you quantify your accomplishments. Make sure there are no errors in spelling or grammar.

> **Resumes need to be quantified and show accomplishments rather than a list of duties and responsibilities.**

Sample resumes can be found in Appendix 2.

Job Interview Preparation

The main purpose of a job interview in Canada is to assess whether the candidate is a "good fit" for the organization.

You must be able to describe your skills, experience and accomplishments in a way Canadian employers can understand.

Canadian employers want their employees to possess skills specific to the job, the occupation and the employer. Employers want you to have transferable soft skills.

> **You may find that the interview questions relate more to your soft skills than your education, occupational skills or work experience.**

When you are contacted for an interview, do your research about the company. Read all documents you can about the company's mission, goals, policies, program and services. Visit the organization before your interview. Walk around the public spaces of the organization to get a sense of how employees dress and interact.

During your interview, you may be asked: *What do you know about this company or why do you want to work here?* The employer is testing you to see if you prepared for the interview by conducting research. It shows that you took initiative and possess research skills.

Canadian employers typically use behavioural interview questions. Behavioural interview questions are used to see if you have the skills and competencies required for the job. They focus more on experiences, behaviours, knowledge, skills and abilities. The best way to prepare for behavioural interview questions is to analyze the job advertisement for skills and attributes the employer is wanting. These are the skills that the interviewers will most likely focus on.

Think about potential interview questions and responses. Your responses must be concise, and to the point, supported by real-life examples.

You may be asked questions about your teamwork skills to determine if you work well with others. If staff will be reporting to you, then expect questions about how you lead, manage and motivate others. You may be asked about how you handled conflict or solved problems or situations.

You may be asked about your strengths and your weaknesses. If you are asked to describe a weakness, state it in a positive way. For example: *I am such a dedicated worker that sometimes I spend too much time on work and not enough time with my family. I have to learn to be more balanced.*

Do research to find examples of behavioural questions you might be asked in your profession.

You will also be asked if you have any questions at the end of the interview, so prepare questions to ask. Do not ask questions about the salary and benefits as these are things you negotiate once you are offered the position.

If you get nervous during interviews, here are two strategies:

- Take a deep breath before you respond to a question
- Ask the interviewer to repeat the question as a tactic to give you more time to think of a response

You are allowed to take documents and notes into an interview. The notes can be reminders of how you plan to answer potential questions. Many settlement agencies offer interview preparation courses that you can attend free of charge.

You want to make a good first impression. Plan what you will wear to the interview. Depending on the occupation, you should dress slightly more formal than what people normally wear to work. Men should wear socks and shoes. Avoid sandals. There is an old rule that says women should only wear white shoes and carry a white handbag from May 24 - September 24.

This rule is not strictly enforced, but for a job interview, you might want to take it under consideration.

Avoid wearing perfume or strong smelling aftershave. Many Canadian workplaces are scent-free.

The best way to answer behavioural interview questions is to use the STAR technique:

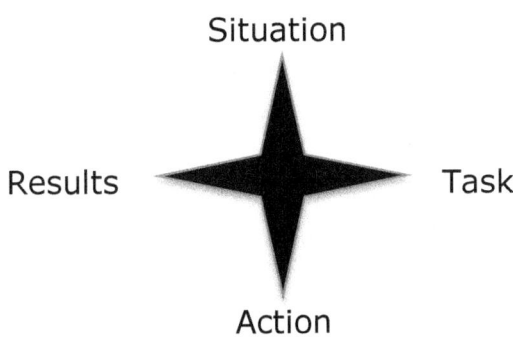

Situation

Results   **Task**

Action

Answer interview questions using the STAR technique:

Situation:	Present a recent situation or challenge you found yourself in.
Task:	Describe what you had to achieve.
Action:	Describe what you did, why you did it and what the alternatives were.
Results:	Present the outcomes of your actions, how you met your objectives, and what you learned from the experience.

Sample Interview Questions and Answers

1. Tell us about yourself.

Answer: The response is job/career related not personal. Make sure you know your resume - you may be asked about skills and experience from previous jobs, which may be more relevant for the role you are interviewing for.

You need to have a short statement prepared in your mind. Be careful that it does not sound rehearsed. Limit it to work-related items unless instructed otherwise. Talk about things you have done, and jobs you have held, that relate to the position you are interviewing for. Start with the item farthest back and work up to the present.

2. What do you know about this company?

Answer: Do as much research as you can about the company. What does it do/sell/make? How many employees work there?

What is its mission and goals? Where does it operate? What are the current issues and who are the major players including competitors? You can insert how your skills and abilities will help the company in their goals and future. These are the key things you should know about a company before going to the interview.

Do the background work, it will make you stand out as someone who comes prepared, and is genuinely interested in the company and the job.

3. *Why do you want to work for us?*

Answer: Here is where you tell them what is great about their organization and link it to your career goals. Your answer should be directly related to the last question. Any research you've done on the company should have led you to the conclusion that you'd want to work there. Put some thought into this answer before you have your interview, mention your career goals and highlight forward-thinking goals and career plans. Do not talk about needing a job, being unemployed, the salary or benefits. Sincerity is extremely important here and will easily be sensed.

4. *What experiences do you have in this field?*

Answer: Speak about specifics that relate to the position you are applying for. If you do not have specific experience, get as close as you can.

5. *In your last position, what were your most significant accomplishments?*

Answer: Always mention a work-related achievement (heading up a successful project or saving the company money is always a good choice), and if you've run a marathon or scaled a mountain, that's an achievement that could be woven into the conversation too.

6. *What are your greatest strengths?*

Answer: Numerous answers are acceptable. Just stay positive. A few good examples: Your ability to prioritize, Your problem-solving skills, Your ability to work under pressure, Your ability to focus on projects, Your professional expertise, Your leadership skills, Your positive attitude, etc.

7. What is your biggest weakness?

Answer: Recognizing the areas in your character and working life that need to be improved is a sign to the interviewer that you are self-aware and strive to progress. If you're asked this question, give a small, work-related flaw that you're working hard to improve. Example: "I've been told I occasionally focus on details and miss the bigger picture, so I've been spending time laying out the complete project every day to see my overall progress."

8. How would your former boss and/or colleagues describe you?

Answer: This is another opportunity to be positive about yourself, so remember to reiterate all your good points especially as they relate to the position you are being interviewed for.

Be prepared with a quote or two from co-workers. Either a specific statement or a paraphrase will work, e.g., One of my co-workers always said I was the hardest worker she had ever known" or even better, "One of my co-workers has always said I was the most reliable, creative problem-solver he'd ever met."

9. Tell us about a problem you had with a supervisor.

Answer: This is a test to see if you will speak ill of your boss. If you fall for it and tell about a problem with a former boss, you may well blow the interview right there. Stay positive and develop a poor memory about any trouble with a supervisor.

10. Describe how you are a team player?

Answer: Be sure to have examples ready. Specifics that show you often perform for the good of the team rather than for yourself are good evidence of your team attitude. Do not brag; just say it in a matter-of-fact tone. This is a key point.

11. Describe a situation where you have ... and how you handled it:

- *Usually these items are taken from the job ad*

- **Example:** *worked under pressure*

Answer: You may say that you thrive under certain types of pressure. Give an example that relates to the type of position applied for.

12. What motivates you to do your best on the job?

Answer: This is a personal trait that only you can say, but good examples are: Challenge, Achievement, and Recognition

13. What qualities do you look for in a boss?

Answer: Be generic and positive. Safe qualities are knowledgeable, a sense of humour, open to new ideas, fair and supportive.

14. What are your goals for the future?

Answer: Employers want to be sure that you won't be moving on to another job right away. The best way to respond to the interview question "What are your goals for the future?" or "Where do you see yourself in five years?" is to refer to the position and the company you are interviewing with. Connect your answer to the job you are applying for. For example, "My long-term goals involve growing with a company where I can continue to learn, take on additional responsibilities and contribute as much value as I can."

15. Why should we hire you?

Answer: Highlight your best points as they relate to the position being discussed. Give a little advance thought to this relationship. Point out how your assets meet what the organization needs. Do not mention any other candidates to make a comparison.

16. What salary do you expect/need?

Answer: Do not answer it as you have already stated this in your cover letter. Instead, say something like, "Can you tell me the range for this position?" In most cases, the interviewer, taken off guard, will tell you. If not, say what you wrote in the cover letter.

17. Any questions for us?

Answer: Remember an interview is a two-way conversation; so be prepared to ask relevant questions. There's no need to wait until the end, feel free to interject with queries and comments as the conversation flows. This will not only give you relevant insight into the organization, it will also help you engage with the interviewer and show that you are confident individual who listens and interacts.

You can show your enthusiasm and interest by discussing aspects of the training programs or talking about the working culture or opportunities for gaining further qualifications. You can ask what a typical career path for someone with your skills and experiences are within the company.

Alternatively, if the interview does not give an opportunity to discuss an aspect of your course, work or extracurricular activities that you feel strongly supports your application, this is an appropriate time to mention it (briefly!).

Job Offer

You are offered a job. Now, it is the time to decide if you accept the job offer. You start by negotiating the salary. Ask what benefits are included. Ask about hours and days of work, policy on overtime, pension plans, professional development and vacations. Ask if you are unionized (union fees will be deducted from your salary). Then, decide if you accept or reject the offer.

If you do not get a job offer after the interview, call or email the HR person or interviewer and ask what you can do to improve your interview skills and other skill areas you need to develop. Thank the person for their feedback and for the opportunity to be interviewed.

Deductions from Your Pay

Pensions

The Canada Pension Plan (CPP) is a program for workers and their families. CPP provides pensions and benefits when contributors retire, become disabled or die. Most individuals who work in Canada contribute to CPP. Your employer will deduct CPP contributions directly from your paycheque. The amount you pay is based on your salary.

Your employer may also have a pension plan that you contribute to each pay period. Deductions will be taken off your paycheque for the company's pension plan.

Taxes

All residents of Canada pay income tax on income they have received throughout the year. Your employer will deduct income taxes directly from your paycheque. The amount of income tax deducted will be based on your salary and family circumstances, i.e., single versus married.

When you file your Income Tax return by April 30th of each year, the government will determine if you paid too much, if so, you will get a refund. If you did not pay enough, then you will be asked to pay more. You can obtain income tax forms at any post office or online.

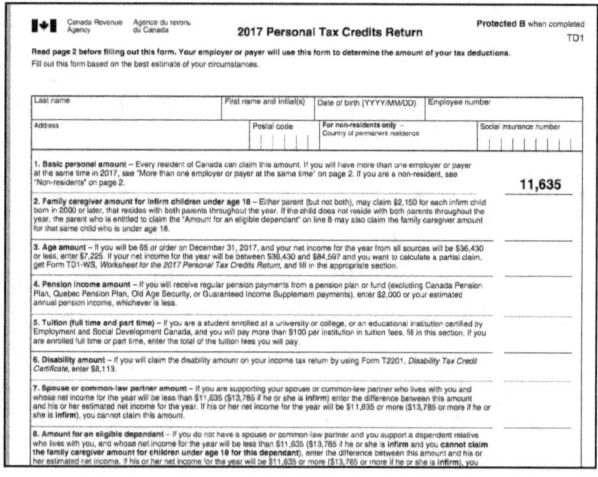

If you leave Canada for an extended period of time, notify the Canadian Revenue Agency, as you may need to file an income tax return for that year.

For more information about taxes, you can ask your employer.

You can contact the Canada Revenue Agency by phone or online at: **www.cra-arc.gc.ca**

You can also register online for a CRA account, which will give you access to your tax information and your Canadian Pension Plan.

Other Deductions

The employer will also deduct from your pay cheque: medical and dental premiums, life insurance premiums, long-term disability premiums, and employment insurance premiums.

Employees' Rights

Knowing your employment and human rights is important once you gain employment.

Employment Standards

In Canada, there are provincial and federal labour laws to protect employees and employers. These laws set minimum wages, hours of work and overtime pay, health and safety standards, parental leave, annual paid vacation, severance pay, meal and coffee breaks, and protection for children. These are described in the Employment Standards for each province and territory and in federal labour standards for those that fall under the federally regulated businesses or industries.

To find out more information online, see the following resources:

Provincial Workplace Standards:
http://www.cic.gc.ca/english/work/labour-standards.asp?_ga=1.16594995.429274252.1464188563

Federal Labour Standards:
https://www.canada.ca/en/employment-social-development/programs/employment-standards.html

---

You have the right to speak up in the workplace when your rights are being violated.

Employers cannot refuse to pay you overtime.

Employers cannot force you to work excessive hours.

Employers cannot fire you or have you deported if you refuse or complain about working overtime or other employee rights that are violated.

Workplace, Health and Safety

All workers in Canada have the right to work in a safe and healthy workplace. Each province and territory as well as the federal government, has its own legislation.

You have the right to refuse unsafe work.

If you become sick or are injured on the job, all provinces and territories provide worker's compensation. You must notify your employer immediately. Contact a physician and file a Worker's Compensation claim with your local workers compensation board.

For more information on Workplace, Health and Safety see:
https://www.canada.ca/en/employment-social-development/programs/health-safety.html

Human Rights

Canada and each of its provinces and territories have human rights laws that prevent employers from discriminating against employees based on gender, age, ethnicity, race, religion, disability or sexual orientation.

Canadian Human Rights Museum, Winnipeg, Manitoba

If you are facing discrimination or harassment in the workplace, the first step is to try to resolve the issue with your employer. You also have the right to file a complaint with your local human rights agency.

> **Your employer cannot discipline you or penalize you for filing a human rights complaint.**

For more information on human rights in your area, see:
www.cashra.ca/links.html

Find a Job Checklist

	To Do	☑
1	Contact Regulatory Body if Profession is Regulated	
2	Identify Your Transferable Skills	
3	Start Building Your Network	
4	Volunteer	
5	Write Cover Letter that is customized to the job advertisement	
6	Write Resume that quantifies your accomplishments	
7	Apply for Jobs	
8	Prepare for Job Interviews	
9	Get help if you need it	
10	Be patient and Do Not Give Up	

CHAPTER 5: CULTURAL DIFFERENCES

Learning to Understand Other Cultures

Canada is a multicultural country with over 200 different languages spoken. Each province also has its own unique culture and sense of identity. Canada is proud of its diversity and its value of being inclusive of all.

Culture is much more than food, dance, song and traditions. Our cultures are formed by our values and beliefs.

There are steps you can take to learn about the cultural differences. The first step is to be aware of your own values, beliefs, assumptions, prejudices and stereotypes. How do each of these affect how you behave and what you think is right or wrong?

The next step is to try to understand the people who you are interacting with and their values, beliefs, assumptions, prejudices and stereotypes. How do each of these affect how they behave and what they think is right or wrong?

Ask questions of others to try to increase your understanding of their culture. Share information about your culture with others.

While you are learning about different cultures in the workplace, watch and observe. Ask questions and mimic others.

Always check your assumptions!

At work and where you live, you will need to have intercultural skills to be successful.

Try the Cultural Quiz to test your intercultural skills.

Cultural Quiz

1. Canadians believe it is acceptable to be a little late for a meeting.

   True   False

2. Business in Canada is more about building relationships as opposed to getting straight down to business.

   True   False

3. Canadians believe that women should take care of family and children.

   True   False

4. French Canadian friends may greet each other by lightly kissing on the cheeks.

   True   False

5. Canadians believe that maintaining eye contact with the person they are speaking with is respectful.

   True   False

6. Canadian managers are expected to manage in an authoritarian manner and employees are expected to unquestioningly follow the manager's suggestions and directions.

   True   False

7. Canadian men may offer their hand to a woman without waiting for her to extend hers first.

   True   False

8. People in Canada expect the right to be heard and listened to in meeting situations regardless of rank or status.

   True   False

9. In Canada, the boss is not expected to perform menial tasks such as making coffee for everybody or moving chairs in a meeting room.

   True   False

10. Gift giving is a tradition in the Canadian workplace.

    True   False

Answers to Cultural Quiz can be found on the next page.

Cultural Quiz Answers

1. false
2. false
3. false
4. true
5. true
6. false
7. true
8. true
9. false
10. false

Are you surprised at the answers?

Culture consists of many components:

- Values
- Interpretations of our perceptions
- Importance placed on time and space
- Childrearing practices
- Gestures
- Social etiquette
- How we grieve
- Systems: political, health, legal, education, social, etc.
- Behaviours
- Dress
- Food and eating habits
- Music and entertainment
- Celebrations

There will always be individual differences but for those who are of the same cultural background, there will be more shared values, behaviours and expectations.

Perceptions and Assumptions

Cultural differences are often misinterpreted. We may be looking at the same thing, but our interpretation of what we see may be very different.

For example, in many Middle Eastern cultures, it is rude and insulting to show the sole of the feet. In Canada, this body language has no meaning.

What happens when two people from these cultures interact and one person shows the sole of his or her feet? One will think nothing of this and the other person might feel he or she is being disrespected.

These two different perceptions and assumptions can affect how people interact in the workplace.

> **As a newcomer to Canada, it is important to learn to check your assumptions about Canadians and about the Canadian workplace.**

Cultural Values and Beliefs

Review some generalized cultural differences between Canada and Syria. Ask yourself: *What are your cultural beliefs and how to you display them through your behavior?*

Values	Canada	Syria
Potentially Different	Individualistic - independent	Collectivist – dependent on group
	Equality - Belief in equity of genders, different sexual orientations and persons with disabilities	Hierarchy – respect for elders
	Gender equity	Gender separation
	Task orientated: Business 1st	Relationship oriented: Friendship 1st
	Structured Time – meet deadlines	Flexible Time - Delays expected and considered normal
	Punctuality highly valued	Rarely on time
	Formal invitations expected	Informal invitations given
	Direct Communication - – Say what you mean and mean what you say	Indirect Communication - nonverbal cues and figurative forms of speech
Similar	Strong work ethic Honesty Diversity	

If Syrian culture is more collectivist, is there a long-term commitment to the family and extended relationships? Is loyalty paramount? Do hiring and promotion decisions take into account family links? Do employees expect to be told what to do by their superiors?

Generally speaking, Syria is considered to be a hierarchical society where subordinates expect to be told what to do by managers. If this is so, how will you deal with a Canadian workplace that is places value on equality? Will you be able to speak up and give your opinion in meetings if your boss is present? Will you be able to call the CEO by his or her first name? Will you be able to change your management style?

In Canada, individual employees and teams are expected to share their expertise with the manager. The manager expects the individual employees to do their jobs, and report if there is a problem that the manager needs to know about. Otherwise, the employee is expected to show initiative and do their jobs with little direction or interference from their superiors.

This is just one of many cultural differences that may create workplace challenges for you and for your Canadian employer.

If you come from a culture where time is flexible and things begin when people arrive, how will you adapt to a Canadian culture that values punctuality? If you come from a culture where women and men socialize separately, how will you handle having a female manager? These are just a few questions to consider.

When you come across behaviours that are unfamiliar or strange to you, ask for clarification. Do not assume and form your perceptions based on what could be a cultural misinterpretation.

CHAPTER 6: CANADIAN WORKPLACE CULTURE

Workplace Culture

You may be asking yourself, "What is workplace culture?"

Workplace culture consists of the values, traditions beliefs, interactions, attitudes, and behaviours considered acceptable at a place of work. It includes how you greet others, your management style, and appropriate topics of conversations, dress code and how employees are treated.

Your goal is to learn the workplace culture of your place of work and behave according to the workplace culture to ensure you are a "fit" for your employer.

To begin to learn about the culture of your workplace, you should read the organization's mission, vision and guiding principle and values. You can also ask for a mentor who is available to help you understand the workplace culture.

Remember, adapting to the Canadian workplace culture simply means adding new ways of thinking, behaving and communicating. By doing this, you will gain an additional way of viewing the world. The more you adapt and learn, the more likely you will succeed in your job in Canada.

Common Cultural Workplace Differences

Every Canadian workplace has its own culture. As a newcomer, you may find that the Canadian workplace culture differs from what you are familiar with in your home country. Canadian workplaces are diverse with people of different ages, genders, sexual orientation, levels of education, and ethnic and cultural backgrounds.

People see the world through their cultural filters. People from two different cultures can view the same behaviour differently. This makes working with different cultures challenging.

There are expected business norms in Canada, and each organization will have its own workplace culture. In order for you to be successful and retain your job, you need to be aware of cultural differences and common business practices.

As a newcomer, you may not have sufficient knowledge and understanding of the Canadian workplace culture, the employer's organizational culture and the Canadian-equivalent culture of your profession or trade.

These are huge barriers for getting hired, retaining a job and being promoted to higher-level positions.

> **In Canada, people are hired for their technical skills and fired for their lack of soft skills and knowledge of the Canadian workplace culture.**

Canadian workplaces vary from organization to organization. The best way to learn the workplace culture is to observe and ask questions. There are some common rules about business etiquette that you can learn.

> **As a newly arrived Syrian refugee, most likely you will not have sufficient knowledge of Canadian culture, workplace culture, the employer's organizational culture and the Canadian-equivalent professional culture of your profession or trade.**
>
> **These are huge barriers for gaining entry into a job, retaining that job and being promoted to higher-level positions.**

Punctuality and Attendance

Generally, business meetings in Canada are well structured and time efficient. Punctuality for meetings, appointments and social events are a highly valued part of Canadian business culture. It is extremely important for you to arrive on time for work or appointments.

If you are delayed more than a couple of minutes, you must inform your supervisor and/or colleagues of the delay and tell them exactly when you will arrive. Then, you must arrive at the said time or inform your colleagues if you are still delayed. If you arrive late, you are expected to quietly and quickly apologize.

Being late is considered rude and disrespectful in Canada. You will be viewed very badly if you are not punctual. In some French-speaking areas, the concept of time is a little more relaxed, but you will still be expected to arrive promptly.

Deadlines are very important and expected to be met as scheduled in Canada. Complete your work on time. If there is a problem, you are expected to inform your supervisor or team lead before the deadline and ask for suggestions, help or an extension. Do not wait until the deadline to apologize after the fact for not completing the work on time. It will not be looked at kindly.

Attendance at work is highly valued by Canadian employers. If you are unable to go to work or a meeting, you must inform your supervisor or the meeting's Chair. Many workplaces have policies on the number of sick days and family days you are allowed to take annually. Some will require a medical certificate to prove that you did not attend work due to illness. It is also inappropriate to leave work early without the approval of your supervisor.

Remember Canada is a country that values "time". As an employee, you need to demonstrate to your employer that you are reliable. This means being on time for work, getting your work done on time and not missing too many days of work.

Privacy and Personal Space

People's privacy and personal space is respected in Canada. Do not ask personal questions about someone's salary or family or personal health. Do not make what is perceived to be a negative comment about someone's appearance or weight. Do not borrow or take an item from someone's office or desk unless you ask beforehand.

Gossiping about others is considered to be very disrespectful.

Personal space comfort level varies across cultures. Standing too close may make the other person feel uncomfortable and standing too far aware is also disconcerting for the other person.

Similar to Syria, about 0.6096 meters or 2 feet (arms-length) is acceptable for business interactions in Canada. In French-speaking areas, the personal space is generally reduced.

Leave Telephone Voice Messages

In Canada, employees schedule their time and are not always available to take your phone calls. You are expected to leave a voice message.

Do not hang up and call several times till you reach the individual. Employers and colleagues find this annoying and rude.

Do not arrive, in person, if whatever you need to communicate can be handled over the telephone or electronically.

Names

In Syria, names are based on the child's first name followed by a middle name, which is usually the father's first name. The family name is often the paternal grandfather's first name or his family name.

In Canada, the given name is the first name. The middle name may be a favourite name of the parents, a family name or the last name of the mother or father. The last name is usually the father's last name but in some cases, it is the mother's last name or a hyphenated name consisting of both the mother and father's last name.

Many Canadian women do not take their husband's name when they marry. Similar to Syria, they keep the full name they were given at birth.

Food and Invitations

Food is very important in both Syrian and Canadian culture.

Eating is an important social activity in Canada. People often invite others for dinner or go out to a restaurant to share a meal. What may be different from your cultural practices is how Canadians deal with invitations, and who pays for the meal.

It is considered polite in Canada to accept the invitation the first time, if one is able to attend. The process of declining the first invitation as a form of politeness does not exist in Canada.

Sharing of food is a common sign of friendship in Syria. Canadian guests will accept food the first time it is offered as in Canada, this would be considered polite.

Canadians, however, do not commonly offer others some of what they are eating unless it is something exceptional, that they want the other person or spouse to experience.

When dining out with friends, it is very common in Canada that the bill for the food will be split for each individual and/or couple. Rarely does the eldest or wealthiest pay for the whole meal. Men do not pay for women's meals unless they are on a romantic date. Friends and colleagues sometimes take turns paying the restaurant bill.

Politeness

Canadians are known for being extremely polite. Words such as, *Please, Thank You, You're Welcome* and *Sorry* are used often. For example, if a Canadian accidentally bumps into someone, both individuals will briefly apologize.

Canadians consider it polite to wait their turn. This applies to all pubic interaction. People will stand in line at cafeteria's, in banks, at grocery stores and at entertainment events.

It is extremely rude to push through people. People are served on a first come, first serve basis. Status, age and gender do not affect who gets served first in Canada.

Soft Skills

Hiring managers want both hard and soft skills in their new hires. It is often said that people are hired for their technical skills but are fired for their lack of soft skills.

Hard skills are job specific. They are the technical skills you possess to be able to do your job. Any shortcomings in hard skills can be learned on the job and through professional development.

Soft skills are essential skills for success in every field of employment. Soft skills such as communication skills, motivation, being a good team player and problem-solving abilities are difficult to teach.

Everyone possesses soft skills. Some are more developed than others. Each person knows what soft skills they should apply in their home country workplaces. For newcomers to Canada, the same soft skills used in their home country may not apply to the Canadian workplace.

Often when newcomers face challenges gaining employment in their profession or miss opportunities for promotions once hired, they resort to taking more education, thinking that by gaining Canadian credentials, it will provide them with more opportunities.

Getting more education is never a bad thing, but it might not get a newcomer that job or promotion they are wanting.

Learning the appropriate soft skills for the Canadian workplace will enhance a newcomer's opportunities for finding professional employment, and being retained and promoted.

Soft skills enable someone to interact constructively and harmoniously with other people. Soft skill abilities improve human performance and facilitate effective interactions amongst people. Other words that are used to describe soft skills include transferable skills, essential skills, emotional intelligence, interpersonal skills and people skills. Soft skills are generally applicable across job titles, professions and industries.

According to Workopolis, the top ten skills requested by prospective Canadian employers are:[58]

1. Communication skills
2. Writing
3. Customer relations
4. Sales
5. Organizational skills
6. Microsoft Office
7. Policy analysis
8. Supervisory skills/leadership
9. Problem solving
10. Teamwork

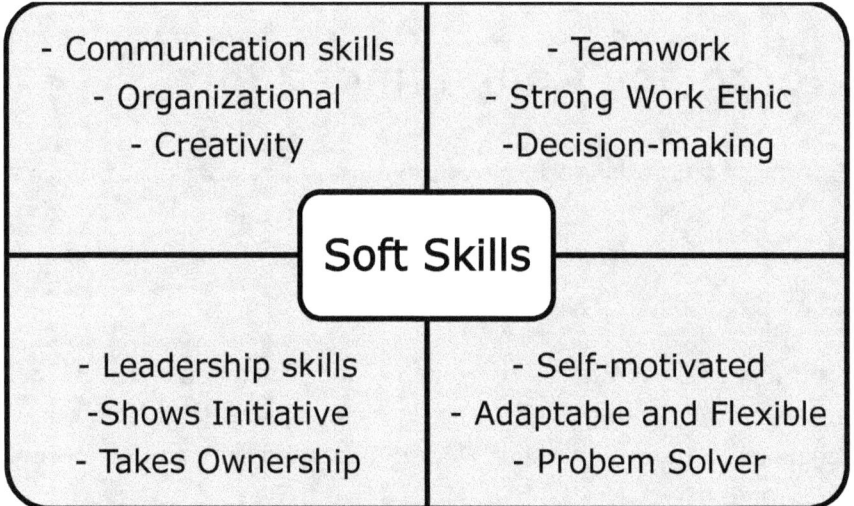

- Communication skills
- Organizational
- Creativity

- Teamwork
- Strong Work Ethic
-Decision-making

Soft Skills

- Leadership skills
-Shows Initiative
- Takes Ownership

- Self-motivated
- Adaptable and Flexible
- Probem Solver

---

[58]http://globalnews.ca/news/2187705/new-study-reveals-top-10-skills-canadian-employers-are-looking-for/

What soft skills are considered to be the most important? The top four soft skills Canadian employers value are:[59]

1. A positive attitude
2. Good communication skills
3. Teamwork skills
4. Strong work ethic (CERIC National Business Survey, 2014)

Other soft skills and attributes Canadian employers look for include active listening skills, initiative, ability to relate to others, patience, open-mindedness, creativity, and proactive problem-solving skills.

See Appendix 3 for a list of Soft Skills.

Workplace Communication

Communication skills are one of the most important skills you need to settle successfully in Canada, and find a good job. They are also considered to be the greatest barrier to success in the Canadian workplace.

Learning to speak English or French clearly is only one part of good communication. Language skills can be learned through language classes and practice. Communication skills can be more challenging.

In Canada, you are eligible for free language classes.

---

[59] http://ceric.ca/career-development-in-the-canadian-workplace-national-business-survey/

Many newcomers, who speak some English or French, make the mistake of thinking that their language skills are adequate, and they immediately start looking for employment. They choose not to attend language classes.

> **You need to have the appropriate language level, understanding of local jargon and professional communication skills to be successful.**
>
> **You may find yourself being unemployed or underemployed if you do not have the language skills employers demand.**

The common measurement tool used in Canada for English language assessment is the Canadian Language Benchmark (CLB) test. For French, the language assessment it is Niveaux de compétence linguistique canadiens (NCLC). Language assessments are free of charge. Your local immigrant-serving agency can refer you for the language assessment test.

To get a good job, generally speaking, you need to score a minimum of CLB or NCLC 7 for speaking, reading, listening and writing. Some professions require a higher language level based on the demands of their occupation. For example, nurses need a higher language level.

If you are below the minimum score in any category, you should strongly consider taking a language class.

> # Do not overestimate your language skills.
>
> # Employers have much higher expectations than immigration officials.
>
> # Employers demand higher-level communication skills.

Communication is more than just speaking a language. It is being able to express yourself effectively, in a manner that is appropriate to the location where you are living. What this means is that you have to be familiar with the local jargon, idioms, colloquial expressions, non-verbal behaviours and humour.

Learning the communication styles of others in the workplace takes time and skills. For example, some supervisors may specifically ask for your input, while others will simply wait for you to express your concerns, if and when they arise.

Communication is multifaceted. It includes non-verbal body language, writing, listening and verbal skills such as public presentation skills.

When employees can communicate effectively and appropriately with co-workers, supervisors and employers, there is a greater likelihood of job retention.

Canadians tend to be less animated than Syrians when speaking. Canadian voices tend to be softer.

Be aware that some Canadians may misinterpret animated conversations using loud voices to signify anger rather than expressive.

Let's look at some common forms of communicating in the Canadian workplace.

Greetings

In Canada, greetings do not hold as much social significance as they do in Syrian culture.

It is common practice to shake hands with people when meeting. When meeting a Canadian business associate or colleague in the workplace, use a firm handshake accompanied by direct eye contact and a sincere smile. When the meeting ends, shake hands once again.

Typically a handshake is no more than three shakes or 2-3 seconds before releasing. Be prepared for men to hold their hand out to shake a woman's hand, as she is considered his equal.

In Quebec only, for both sexes, people kiss once on each cheek when they greet one another. This is uncommon for non-French Canadians. Colleagues sometimes hug if they know each other well and have not seen each other for a long time.

Unlike in Syrian culture, Canadians do not place their right hand on their heart when meeting someone as a way of expressing affection.

For initial introductions, use the appropriate professional title such as "Dr." or "Ms.", or "Mr." followed by the last name. Most likely you will quickly be invited to use first names.

Syrians of the same sex are often quite physical with each other when greeting. Holding hands, kissing cheeks and touching one another's face or shoulders is common. Canadians of the same sex do not greet each other in this manner.

When Canadians greet, they commonly say, "Good Morning". It is appropriate for you to also say, "Good Morning". Another common way that Canadians greet is to say, "Hi. How are you?" They are not expecting you to reply with how you actually feel. This expression is simply a greeting. The common response is, "Good" or "Not Bad".

Unlike Syria, Canadian greetings are not lengthy, and usually do not include questions about health, unless someone has been ill. Then, one might ask if they are feeling better.

The custom in Canadian workplaces is to greet people in the hallway and when you arrive or leave work with *hello, good morning* or *good night*. It is polite to greet all co-workers and managers regardless of their position in the organization.

It is common when meeting business associates at a meeting or leaving a meeting to shake hands. Canadian men and women shake hands, even if they are not related.

Eye Contact

Similar to Syria, in Canada, making direct eye contact with the other speaker shows that you are interested and paying attention.

Staring or making limited eye contact is considered rude in Canada. You are expected to make eye contact when you are speaking with someone, including someone who is your superior such as a boss.

Typically, Canadians look at the person for three seconds, quickly and briefly look away, and then repeat.

Lack of eye contact in Canada is interpreted in many different ways. You may be considered shy, nervous or embarrassed. You may be considered a liar and dishonest or someone that has something to hide. Individuals may think you lack confidence or are distracted. These are just some of the assumptions people might make about you, if you do not make, the expected eye contact in Canada.

If you are uncomfortable making eye contact, practice with your family members or friends.

Direct versus Indirect Communication

Generally speaking, Anglo Canadians tend to be direct communicators. They value efficiency in communication and honesty over personal sensitivities. Saying, "No" or "I don't know" is considered to be respectful and honest.

Direct Communicators say exactly what they think. They use clear, definitive statements. Participate actively in meetings. Use words like "should" and "have to". They are comfortable telling others why their ideas should be adopted.

In Syrian culture where indirect communication is expected, directly communicating negative information may be seen as impolite and rude. In business situations, polite excuses or evasions and outright fictions are considered to be diplomatic and appropriate strategies.

If you are an indirect communicator, you may find yourself asking a lot of questions, quietly observing in meetings and offering suggestions for consideration. You may use words such as "maybe" and "possibly". You tend to ask others to consider your ideas.[60]

Being a direct communicator at work is expected in Canada. If you are unsure, ask for clarification. It's better to be clear on expectations now than to try to fix a problem later.

Learn to say "NO' or "I don't know" rather than making a commitment you cannot fulfil.

---

[60] Adapted from:
http://www.yourofficecoach.com/topics/coworker_relationships/personality_differences/are_you_a_direct_or_indirect_communicator.aspx

> It is acceptable to say, *"No, I do not understand"*.

Speak Up at Work

In the Canadian workplace, you are expected to speak up, ask questions and share your ideas. For Canadian supervisors, this indicates that you are interested and want to be involved. Do not worry whether you have perfect English or an accent. Everyone has an accent. It is more important to show that you are participating than to remain silent.

Learn to participate in meetings and group discussions. Give your opinion on the topic or project. Ask questions for clarification and when you do not understand directions.

At meetings and when having discussions with team members, it is considered courteous in Canada to wait your turn to speak. Interrupting someone while they are talking is considered to be rude.

Common Canadian Gestures

The meaning of gestures is very different across cultures. To avoid misinterpretation, it is very important to learn the meaning of gestures used in Canada.

Thumbs Up

Thumbs Up in Canada is a sign of approval. It means great or okay.

Raising Your Eyebrows

In Canada, raising one's eyebrows means "What?" or "Really?" It does not mean "No".

Feet Placement

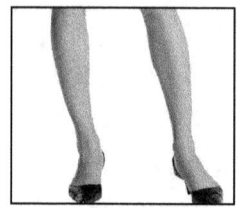

Pointing feet or toes directly at someone has no meaning in Canada. It is not considered to be negative, rude or an insult.

Hand Over Heart

Placing your hand over your heart expresses sincerity in some parts of the world. In Canada, this gesture has similar meaning but is not commonly used.

Come Here

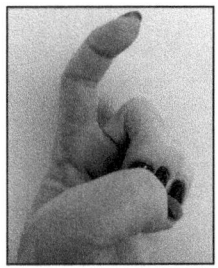

In Canada, this gesture is used to motion someone to come over.

Same Gender Holding Hands

Same gender holding hands is not a common sign of friendship in Canada. It typically indicates that the pair is a romantic couple.

Okay Sign

Forming circle with thumb and pointer finger indicates satisfaction in Canada.

Downward Palm Wave

This gesture is used to shoo someone away in Canada. It does not mean "come here".

If you are unsure about different gestures, ask for clarification. You can also mirror the person with who you are talking with. This means adopting body language and expressions similar to the sender.

Touch

Canadians generally do not touch one another or hold hands in the workplace. The only conventional touch is a handshake. You need to be mindful of, and sensitive to, others' tolerance for touch.

In Canada, it is acceptable for men and women to hold hands or link arms. This typically occurs in a romantic relationship.

In Syria, men may hold hands or link arms with other men and women may link arms or hold hands with other women as a sign of friendship.

In Canada, men do not commonly hold hands or link arms with other men nor do women commonly hold hands or link arms with other women as a sign of friendship.

In Canada, same-sex couples hold hands or link arms. However, you may also observe women dancing together at social events in rural areas and small towns in Canada. This has nothing to do with their sexuality.

Common Canadian Terms and Idioms

Every country and language has its own jargon and colloquial expressions. Unless you understand the terms and idioms used in Canada, and in your profession, you will not be proficient and effective in your profession.

> **Idioms are phrases, which people use in everyday language, which do not make sense, but are understood.**

Your profession may also use acronyms and technical terms that may be unfamiliar to you. It is important to learn and understand these terms for you to be successful in your career.

> **When you hear an expression, idiom or phrase that you do not understand, ask what the other speaker is trying to say.**

A list of some common Canadian terms and idioms can be found in Appendix 4.

Role of Supervisors

The supervisor - subordinate relationship may be different from what you are accustomed to in Syria. In the Canadian workplace, supervisors guide and mentor employees, resolve conflict, and support the team whenever necessary.

Supervisors are expected to have leadership skills to manage their staff. They do not have, to have, better technical skills than their staff.

Supervisors in Canada put a great deal of trust in their team members to use their own thinking, ask questions, speak up and show initiative. Individuals and team members do not rely on supervisors to provide explicit directions or to micro-manage them.

Supervisors usually do not have enough time to do everything. This means they want you to do, what you can, without them. In other words, they want you to be in charge of your own work. They do not want you to sit at your desk waiting for them to tell you what to do. They expect you to know when to act independently and when to ask them first. Do not depend on your supervisor to tell you what to do, when to do it or how to do it.

Remember you are paid for your skills and for your ideas. Your supervisor doesn't have all the solutions to problems. You are paid to contribute ideas and to speak up when you disagree. When you say nothing, colleagues, team members and supervisors may think you don't understand, you don't care, or you are too shy. Your team expects you to speak up.

Relationships at Work

In Canada, relationships at work are for business-purposes. You are expected to get down to (conduct) business rather than build relationships. Your age, gender, education, past or present job titles are irrelevant when it comes to building relationships in the Canadian workplace.

> **Trust is built by doing what you say you will do.**
>
> **Credibility comes from doing a job well.**

People are friendly but are not usually your friends. Although you may share life stories and experiences, socialize at work events and help each other, at the end of the day these are your colleagues. Only a small number may end up being your friends outside of work.

It is however very important to build and maintain relationships at work. This is part of teamwork.

Here are some things you can do to accomplish this:

- Listen to and respectfully acknowledge the concerns, issues, ideas and opinions of others,
- Ask for clarification when you do not understand or know what is being discussed,
- Complete your work on time,
- Notify others on your team if there are delays, changes or problems in a timely manner,
- Support others in achieving team goals by assisting team members solve challenges,
- Share credit with team members,
- Use only English or French at work, including when socializing with same-language co-workers, and
- Participate in social events at work.

Informality

As already noted, Canadians value equality. Business relationships are not viewed by order of rank, status, position or gender. As a result, interactions between a manager and a subordinate are largely informal.

Managers delegate and share power. In meetings, Canadians will expect everyone to participate and contribute to discussions from junior through to senior colleagues. They will not wait for their superior to tell them what to do. Employees are expected to take initiative, be self-directed and work with minimal guidance from above.

Managers and subordinates socialize together. Woman and men are treated equally. Age is irrelevant. Employees, supervisors, managers, directors and CEOs call each other by their first names.

Socializing and Small Talk

Small talk and socializing is common in the Canadian workplace. What is small talk? It is polite conversation about unimportant or uncontroversial matters such as the weather.

Small talk is usually conducted when waiting for people to arrive at a meeting, when walking somewhere together, during breaks and sometimes when one first arrives in the workplace.

As Canadians tend to be more task-oriented, do not expect lengthy small talk during business. In fact, engaging in long conversations during office hours is not considered to be appropriate in the Canadian workplace.

In many Canadian workplaces, there is a strong division between home and work life. Talk about family is limited. Small talk is usually about the weather, traffic, sports and what you did on weekends or vacations. People rarely ask personal questions such as, "What is your salary?" or "What is your religion?" When conducting small talk avoid discussing religion, politics, income, weight and age.

It is very important to participate in small talk in the Canadian workplace. It shows that you are interested in others, builds rapport and strengthens teams.

Avoid just congregating with people from your own culture during breaks. This can appear snobbish or rude to others. When you are at the workplace, it is important for you to be inclusive of others and build your network.

If you do not know what co-workers are talking about, fake it by asking questions about their topic: *Where is that restaurant? What kind of food do they serve? What hockey teams were playing? What was the final score?*

The other speakers will be unaware that you do not know what to say. They will appreciate your participation.

Take Initiative

Canadian employers expect you to be a self-starter and express your opinions and ideas. Someone who shows initiative is considered to be proactive, persistent and flexible.

Showing initiative means taking action in the workplace without being told what to do. Showing initiative is important in the Canadian workplace as it demonstrates your value at work and your capacity to develop as a leader.

Show initiative by:

- being a self-starter (a person who begins work or undertakes a project on his or her own initiative, without needing to be told or encouraged to do so),

- using a proactive approach to work (you act rather than react at work),

- becoming more flexible and adaptable,

- being able to anticipate what needs to be done and doing it,

- being able to evaluate a situation or problem and then doing something about it,

- being persistent in overcoming challenges that arise in pursuit of the end goal,

- being creative,

- constantly searching for new solutions and more effective approaches,

- doing more than is required of you,

- speaking up and sharing your ideas,

- thinking as a team member and not as an individual employee, and

- making suggestions on how to do things better.

In the Canadian workplace, you will need to find out how much you can do by yourself (initiate), and when you need to ask (get permission) to do something. People often use initiative when they have to solve a problem, make a decision or plan a job task.

Demonstrating Initiative Checklist

Make it your goal to find out when you need to use initiative and when you need to ask your supervisor.

The following checklist will help you assess how well you demonstrate initiative:

	Demonstrating Initiative Checklist	✔
1.	Know how things work and how you can improve them. Observe everything going on around you. Be curious and ask questions. Analyze each situation.	
2.	Constantly search for new solutions and more effective approaches, i.e., simplify processes, ways to save money and reduce costs, etc.	
3.	Stay alert to find new and better ways of doing things.	
4.	Think ahead and anticipate likely challenges with well-planned deliverable actions. As problems arise, take action and deal with them immediately.	
5.	Be prepared, i.e., read materials in advance, research the project, etc.	
6.	Provide, in advance, the answers to the questions you know are going to be asked.	
7.	At team meetings always share your ideas and opinions.	
8.	Help your team members share ideas by asking them questions. Listen to them carefully.	
9.	Speak up. Proactively suggest improvement ideas to colleagues, team members and supervisors, and at internal and external meetings.	

	Demonstrating Initiative Checklist	✔
10.	Do not wait for your supervisor to tell you what to do next. Begin new tasks before being told.	
11.	Think of yourself as a team member. You are one part of the project and each team member relies on you to do his or her job well. Ask your co-workers about how your work impacts their work. Pay attention to each detail and component of the project including the timeline for each team member.	
12.	Look for work to fill any spare time. Do not wait for someone else to tell you what to do.	
13.	Try to do something extra all the time. Make yourself available for extra tasks or overtime.	
14.	Use your time efficiently. Do the most important jobs first. Then, when colleagues and/or team members need you unexpectedly, you can help them.	
15.	Keep communication with superiors open.	
16.	Work independently. However, if you are unsure about something or you do not understand, always ask your supervisor or someone on your team.	
17.	Volunteer for challenging projects, assignments and committee work.	
18.	Be self-confident. Know that you have creative ideas.	

In the Canadian workplace, you will need to find out how much you can do by yourself (initiate), and when you need to ask (get permission) to do something. People often use initiative when they have to solve a problem, make a decision or plan a job task.

Develop Your Initiative Skills

Initiative is an essential skill that you can develop and grow. You can do this by following these steps:

1. **Set Small Goals**

   Set small goals so you can achieve some quick wins. Push yourself to do things that you might be scared to do.

2. **Detect Opportunities and Potential Improvements**

   Always be on the lookout for areas in your work, team, projects and company that could use improvement. Look for opportunities for improvement that your colleagues or superiors have not noticed. Keep your mind open to new ideas and new possibilities.

   Keep these questions in mind when looking for opportunities for improvement:
   - What would our customers want us to improve?
   - How can we improve quality?
   - What small problems, issues, difficulties or challenges exist that could become bigger?
   - What slows our work or makes it more difficult?
   - What is frustrating for our team?

3. Show Initiative

Share your ideas for improvement with your colleagues, team and superiors and act on them using the following steps:

I. Identify what needs improvement,

II. Identify a solution,

III. Conduct research,

IV. Identify costs and assess risks associated with your idea for improvement,

V. If costs and risks are minimal, consider going ahead with your idea directly, while keeping your supervisor informed of your idea and actions, and

VI. If costs and risks are significant, prepare a written plan and ask for authorization before proceeding.

4. Provide Updates

Team members are expected to provide updates about the progress of their work on a project during a team meeting or a meeting with the supervisor. You are expected to share what you are doing, the progress of the project including what is not completed and any problems and/or challenges that have occurred. Updates are also an opportunity to show initiative by including your suggestions on how to do something more effectively and/or more efficiently. Try to use approximately the same amount of time or less, than your colleagues, use when providing updates.

Be proactive and prepare your updates in advance of any team/supervisor meetings. Keep track of your updates on an Excel sheet and/or Word document.

Depending on your company's workplace culture, you might also want to consider providing your colleagues, team members and/or supervisor with a written copy of your updates.

A guideline to prepare your oral update is to ask yourself how much time you have to provide your update. For example, if you only have three minutes, what does your team/supervisor need to know? How can you support your main point and do this within three minutes?

Take Ownership

In the Canadian workplace, taking ownership is one of the most important roles in project management. Taking ownership is where one believes that taking action is not someone else's responsibility.

Taking ownership is not just doing a job, or working on a project, it means making it your mission to see it through to completion. The basic idea is that the company wants each team member emotionally invested in making whatever it is happen, working whatever hours and schedules are needed, sacrificing other activities, etc. to reach the end goal on time.

Team members who take ownership are both willing and capable of adapting to a delayed or failing project, both in their plan and in their role itself. They do what it takes to get the project back on track (to stay on the path that one is on; to continue doing the things one is doing).

Team members take ownership when they believe that taking action is not someone else's responsibility. They believe that each team member is accountable for the quality and timeliness of an outcome and the end product.

Taking ownership is showing initiative and being accountable to follow-through. It's not just about the individual team member and their goals or commitments, it's about acknowledging that their actions affect other team members' abilities to accomplish their goals.

Taking ownership means when you have part of a project to complete, you will deliver as promised, on time and within budget. It also means that you will be forthcoming when you fall short (to lack enough of something; to not reach an amount or standard; to fail to attain a specified amount, level, or degree; to prove inadequate).

If the individual team member cannot deliver on time or the results will not be as perfect and complete as hoped, the individual team member should be honest and communicate this to team members and/or supervisors. By acknowledging that their actions affect other team members' abilities to accomplish their goals, the individual team member is showing respect to the team.

> **Being accountable is a major factor in building trust in the Canadian workplace.**

Taking ownership tells other team members that the individual team member can be trusted to do the right thing; they are going to do what they say, and come back with results. It means the individual team member will not let the team down (disappoint the team).

Low trust translates to poor productivity. If supervisors and team members do not trust each other, then time is wasted following up and managing details that are not their responsibility.

Taking ownership means standing up and announcing that you are responsible for executing a particular task or project. It means making an active and enthusiastic commitment. Sometimes taking ownership will just mean being accountable for a project within your job description. But, it can mean doing things outside your job description or assigned part of a project. It can mean helping your team members with their assigned roles. It can mean doing menial tasks that require your department to function efficiently. It means making suggestions for improvements. It means observing what needs to be done and doing it for the greater good of the project and the company.

When you take ownership, you establish your reputation as a problem solver. Taking on more tasks from menial to large scale differentiates you from other employees and forces you to continuously learn new things. It diversifies what you do and it creates job security. You express yourself as a leader that can be depended upon when there are tasks to be done, problems to be solved and solutions to be found.

Why Do Managers Want Employees to Take Ownership?

Managers like to see their employees own a project, process and/or job because it means that they care. The employees have moved beyond just coming to work. They now want to see the project succeed.

When employees take ownership of their work, they treat the business they are working for as if it were their own. The employees will be more driven, motivated, and have more initiative. They will seek creative and innovative ways to improve and develop what they are doing. They go beyond just fulfilling only the minimum requirements of the job.

A company with employees who take ownership is a company that's moving forward. This is highly valued in the Canadian workplace.

This next checklist provides an opportunity for you to self-assess your skills at taking ownership.

Take Ownership Checklist

	Actions	✔
1.	You take responsibility for the project.	
2.	You volunteer to lead the project to completion.	
3.	You let your supervisor know that you are there to help.	
4.	You take the lead and drive the direction on how the situation should be handled.	
5.	You are a learner - when new situations arise, you automatically learn something new.	
6.	You are a team player - you have to coordinate with different people across different teams.	
7.	You always view yourself as a "business partner" and not just the job listed on your job description.	
8.	You use your skills to be a "business partner" not just an employee.	
9.	You persevere - you are hardworking and have a great attitude.	
10.	You are an honest communicator.	
11.	You gather information and complete the research to understand all the parameters of the project.	
12.	You work with your team if there are multiple areas that require research.	
13.	You create an outline of the project's goals and objectives.	
14.	You list the steps that require completion to ensure project success.	

	Actions	✓
15.	You create a project timeline including a schedule that includes the dates when specific project aspects require completion.	
16.	You assign tasks and duties to project team members and/or yourself.	
17.	You develop reports and a reporting structure that keeps everyone on the team in the loop (having knowledge and information about the specific project) as to the project status.	
18.	You create reports for your supervisor to review that make it easy for her/him to stay apprised of project goals, completed tasks and objectives, and outcomes.	
19.	You do not look to others to address issues; instead you look for problems before they become obvious, and find and implement solutions.	
20.	You know when you cannot fix a problem you will find the person who can fix it, and make sure they address the issue.	
21.	You are proactive about finding and solving problems.	
22.	You practice continual contingency planning and adapt quickly to challenges and setbacks.	
23.	You are willing to do what it takes to get the job done.	
24.	You hold and/or attend regular project meetings.	
25.	You are flexible and are willing to step into a different role or take on other responsibilities to accomplish project goals and timelines.	
26.	You avoid taking the credit for your part of the project.	
27.	You recognize team members who contributed to the project's success.	
28.	You are comfortable acting with increasing autonomy and decreased oversight.	

Expectations of Honesty and Integrity

Canadian employers value honesty. You are expected to tell your supervisor when you do not understand, are uncertain about directions, cannot do the task or cannot meet the deadline.

"Yes" in Canada means you understand and will act. If you come from a culture where communication is more indirect, you may find it difficult to say "No" to a manager or superior.

Replying with a comment such as, "I will do my best" is considered to be a "Yes", I will do the task and meet the deadline.

The expression, *honesty is the best policy*, is highly valued in Canada. It means you are expected to tell the truth, even when it seems it would be useful to lie or apologize later.

Canadians expect you to say "no" if you cannot accomplish a task or meet deadlines. They do not want you to apologize or make excuses for incomplete work.

You are not expected to tell the boss what you think s/he wants to hear.

You are expected to be honest and act with integrity.

Performance Evaluation and Constructive Criticism

"Constructive criticism is the process of offering valid and well-reasoned opinions about the work of others, usually involving both positive and negative comments, in a friendly manner rather than an oppositional one. The purpose of constructive criticism is to improve the outcome."[61]

In Canada, constructive criticism is considered to be part of the growth and professional development of employees. It is delivered in a calm manner with the expectation that the person receiving the criticism will respond in a professional manner.

These are the five steps to giving constructive criticism:

1. Start with something positive.
2. Be constructive, specific, helpful and sensitive.
3. Refer to the person's behaviour or the specific situation, not the person.
4. Invite a collaborative discussion of the consequences.
5. Focus on behaviours that the other person can improve.

This is how you should receive constructive criticism from others:
- Recognize the value of the feedback.
- Do not become defensive or be offended.
- Respect, accept and consider.
- Resolve any misunderstandings.
- Thank the other person for the feedback.
- Use the constructive criticism to improve.

---

[61] https://en.wikipedia.org/wiki/Constructive_criticism

Speaking Your First Language at Work

Speaking your first language with colleagues from your home country sometimes creates an uncomfortable work environment for non-speakers.

You do have the right to speak in your own language when not dealing directly with clients or customers. However, be aware that some of your colleagues may feel left out or think you are ridiculing them, if you only associate with co-workers from your own culture.

You need to be able to determine when it is appropriate to speak your first language when you are at work. What you do on your meal and coffee breaks is your business. However, if you have colleagues who join you on your break who do not understand your language, speak in the language that everyone understands. This is simply being respectful.

Let your co-workers know ahead of time, that you need some downtime and it is more relaxing to speak in your first language during breaks.

Do not exclude others.

Avoid speaking in your first language when working. Co-workers who do not speak your language often perceive it negatively.

Discrimination and Racism

In Canada, there are human rights laws to address discrimination and racism, and a constitutional guarantee of equal rights for all. If you experience racism or discrimination in the workplace, most workplaces have respectful workplace policies and procedures to deal with such behaviours.

Each province also has a Human Rights Commission where you can file a report if you are discriminated against.

There are seven discriminatory practices prohibited by the Canadian Human Rights Act[62]:

- "Denying someone goods, services, facilities or accommodation.
- Providing someone goods, services, facilities or accommodation in a way that treats them adversely and differently.
- Refusing to employ or continue to employ someone, or treating him or her unfairly in the workplace.
- Following policies or practices that deprive people of employment opportunities.
- Paying men and women differently when they are doing work of the same value.
- Retaliating against a person who has filed a complaint with the Commission or against someone who has filed a complaint for them.
- Harassing someone."

---

[62] Canadian Human Rights Act, http://www.chrc-ccdp.ca/eng/content/what-discrimination

Regardless of the law, you are bound to experience racism and discrimination in your daily lives. You may face greater surveillance by the police. You may earn less income, regardless of your education and experience. You may overhear people making comments about what you wear, particularly for women. You may hear comments about being Muslim, Jewish, etc. This can be very stressful!

Try not to become depressed, bitter, angry or hurt. The best way to deal with racism and discrimination is to report it to your employer.

If you are confronted with discrimination or racism in your daily personal life, do not confront the person with anger. If you have a relationship with whoever is making the comment, then try to educate. If it is a stranger, you can either ignore the comment or politely reply. If it is an authority figure such as a police officer, then remain calm, do as you are told and then afterwards, report the incident to the Police Chief.

The best way to confront racism is to get involved in community activities that educate others about discrimination and racism. You will have a much better and broader impact. It is a way of turning something negative into something positive.

In Conclusion

Settlement assistance is available to you. Language training is available to you. Use both these opportunities to help you learn English or French and to settle successfully in Canada.

Integration is a process that will take many years to achieve. Ask questions when you do not understand something or are unsure of how to proceed. Get help when you are feeling depressed or sad or isolated.

Spend time with your family doing things that you enjoy. Spend time with other people from your home country. Spend time with people in your religious communities. Spend time becoming friends with people who are Canadian-born. Be active.

Check your assumptions. What you perceive may be an incorrect assumption, as you are in a new country and a new culture.

Remember that everyone has an accent. Remember why you chose to come to Canada. Remember that Canada wants you to feel welcome.

Be patient! Be curious! Do not give up! Ask for help when you are unsure or feel lost or lonely.

Help is available!

Welcome to your new home!

APPENDICES

Appendix 1: Sample Cover Letters

Job: Administrative Officer

NAME

Street Address, City, Province, Postal Code

• Telephone Number   • Email address

Date

Person's Name of who cover letter should be sent
Title
Organization's Name
Street Address
City, Province, Postal Code

RE: Job Posting Title, Advertisement Number if stated

Dear Sir or Madam,

I am applying for the Administrative Officer for *Company Name*. I am extremely interested in this position as it perfectly fits my experience. For the past ten years, I have provided office management, and financial and administrative services to various organizations. As you can see in the chart below, my education and work experience qualifies me for the Administrative Officer position.

Job Requirements	My Qualifications
Must be legally entitled to work in Canada.	I am a Permanent Resident qualified to work in Canada.
Valid full class 5 Manitoba driver's license	I have a valid full class 5 Manitoba driver's license.

Experience in administrative and office management	As an Operations Manager in my current position, I oversee all business and highly confidential company matters including human resource management, vendor identification, procurement and management, facilities management, product purchasing and insurance, SEO, advertising, financial and accounting matters and legal compliance. This demonstrates my experience in administrative and office management.
Experience in managing staff and coordinating work	I currently supervise and coordinate the work of over 40 employees for 4 companies at 2 different locations. This includes supervising managers, accounting, service and sales staff.
Experience monitoring, preparing, coordinating, and maintaining financial information, including operational budgets, forecasting, variance reporting, and coding of payables	I currently forecast, prepare and monitor the budgets of 3 companies. I have reviewed and authorized over 2000 new loan applications for the purchase of vehicles, audited over 4000 sale files to ensure correct documentation and investigated audit defects.
Ability to develop and implement efficient administrative processes	I develop, implement and ensure compliance with administrative processes for my current employer including all HR policies and procedures.
Experience working with electronic accounting/financial software	I have experience using Simply Accounting and am able to learn new software applications relatively quickly.

| Excellent verbal and written communication skills as well as strong interpersonal and customer service skills | I have demonstrated my strong communication skills, both verbal and written, throughout my career. In my various roles, I regularly liaised with customers, co-workers and vendors.

Verbal: In my current role, I handle all matters pertaining to the Better Business Bureau and Consumer Protection Office from customer complaints to release of documents. This role requires strong diplomacy and an ability to communicate common goals to diverse individuals and organizations.

Written: An example of my written communication skills in one of my roles was to prepare over 500 documents of transfer, 100 legal documents and 150 proof of claims for bankruptcies.

Interpersonal: I currently arrange and coordinate corporate events for customers and staff. Using my planning and organizational skills, I design the event, book space and interact with vendors. During the event, I interact with customers on a one-to-one basis. |
| Excellent verbal and written communication skills as well as strong interpersonal and customer service skills | Customer Service: I have worked as frontline staff where I greeted and directed about 100 people per day. Currently, I resolve customer issues ensuring that their needs are met. |

Strong problem solving skills	Problem solving is one of my strengths and I use this skill daily. I report directly to the company's President and am the primary decision-maker for operational matters. This includes resolving problems managers face with staff and customers, handling computer software issues and dealing with vendor concerns. One of my primary goals and expertise is to resolve problems so that the needs of the company are met while at the same time ensuring that an effective resolution is found for staff, customers and vendors.
Ability to prioritize a high volume of workload to meet deadlines with accuracy and strict attention to detail	Working in a fast-paced environment, with a multitude of diverse responsibilities, it is imperative that I am able to meet deadlines with accuracy and provide accurate details. For each step of the purchase of the product, I conduct the advertising, review loan application and legal documentation, monitor the budget inventory, plan sales events and arrange facilities, each of which must be met on a schedule.
Supervisory experience in a unionized environment	Although I have no direct experience supervising in a unionized environment, I know that successful labour relations starts with establishing good relationships with employees. From my current experience supervising staff, developing good communications with employees is an important step in developing trust and respect, which leads the way to successful labour relations.

I look forward to being interviewed where I can share my experience, strengths and abilities in more detail.

Thanks you for your consideration.

Yours sincerely,
Signature

Name

NAME

Street Address, City, Province, Postal Code

• Telephone Number   • Email address

Date

Person's Name of who cover letter should be sent
Title
Organization's Name
Street Address
City, Province, Postal Code

RE: Job Posting Title, Advertisement Number if stated

Dear Sir or Madam,

Twenty-one years experience in accounting and finance with a proven track record in managing the general ledger and financial reporting, administering accounting systems, developing annual budgets and forecasting, while building and maintaining positive relationships with internal and external clients, are just part of the knowledge I would bring to your position of Manager of Finance. I am a goal-oriented, self-starter who began as a volunteer in a similar non-profit community service society and within five months was employed in the accounting department of that same agency.

My extensive knowledge of accounting systems is important because I can spearhead the implementation of these systems to save money and improve accuracy. One of my recent accomplishments included initiating a comprehensive income and expense analysis that proved for early identification and correction of a posting error reducing 20% of month-end time and improving accuracy by 90%. Additionally, when I was preparing tax rebate applications, I noticed $120,000 of missing money owed to the agency. I also developed complex financial reports for forecasting, trending and results analysis that tracked lost money and showed proper invoicing.

During the course of my career, I have gained a specialist's understanding of financial instruments and accounting software and have also been effective in explaining complex information in a comprehensible manner. I am relied upon to convey essential financial data to all levels of management and external stakeholders, including advice on the auditing processes. I liaise with federal and provincial governments and 20 community agencies on financial and administrative functions and concerns, billing matters and contract changes. These include some of the same funders and partners as your organization, such as Citizenship and Immigration Canada, Ministry of Children and Family Services and the United Way, making me familiar with budget processes, grant applications, monitoring and reporting policies and procedures. My ability to be an effective communicator in dealing with staff, management and external funders, vendors and partners is the strength of my financial leadership.

My analytic, time-management and communication skills are excellent allowing me to meet cyclical deadlines and manage the numerous duties of the Manager of Finance with ease. I am meticulous when it comes to details and rarely make an accounting error.

My key accounting and financial competencies include, but are not limited to, bookkeeping, payroll, deferred revenue and accounts receivable schedules, account reconciliation, cash flow, preparation of accounting and financial reports and statements, budget monitoring systems maintenance, resource and expense tracking systems, resolution of any escalated vendor disputes and billing charges, monitoring and analysis of general ledger account and preparation of annual audit documentation, and provision of financial support. Currently, I train, lead and oversee the work of a 3-person accounting team and coordinate pay and benefits information flow to 80 employees. I have worked closely with all managers, in particular the Director of Human Resources, and am familiar with human resource policies and practices.

My experience and skills will enable me to make a valuable contribution to *Name of Organization* as Manager of Finance, and it would also be gratifying to be able to support and be part of an organization that promotes excellence and creates a culture of continuous improvement within business functions and program areas.

I will bring not only my years of expert experience but also my personal drive for results and positive outcomes. I am prepared for the next challenge in my career and look forward to an interview to discuss my qualifications more fully.

Sincerely,
Signature

Name

NAME

Street Address, City, Province, Postal Code

• Telephone Number   • Email address

Date

Person's Name of who cover letter should be sent
Title
Organization's Name
Street Address
City, Province, Postal Code

RE: Job Posting Title, Advertisement Number if stated

Dear (Insert Mr. or Ms. Last Name or Sir and/or Madam):

As a seasoned, 10-year hospitality management professional with a proven track record of overseeing operations of 6 dining outlets with a 350-seat capacity in a 5-Star luxury 218-room hotel that serves 369,000 annually, this is what I would offer your hotel. I have experience working in the hotel industry under three different international hospitality brands, *LIST BRANDS* and have been promoted and consistently entrusted with large operational agendas throughout my employment. Currently, I lead a combined staff of 90, which also encompasses hiring, staff training, career coaching, scheduling, mentoring and evaluation. I strongly believe that my professional experience, educational background and track record align with the qualities and capabilities of the individual you are seeking to lead your operations to superior financial performance and exceptional guest satisfaction.

I have a Master's degree in Tourism Management with proven experience in hotel food and beverage operation management, customer service and team management. For the and past 6 years, I have been the Assistant Food and Beverages Manager at the *Name Hotel*. I am results-oriented with strong leadership and interpersonal skills, effective organizational and planning skills, exceptional customer service skills and excellent budgetary, projection and cost control skills ensuring the highest level of guest satisfaction at all times.

I have very strong verbal skills with the ability to communication effectively with staff members, executives, guests and vendors. I have strong problem solving skills and the ability to make good decisions while working under pressure in a fast-paced hotel environment while exceeding guest and company expectations. I always maintain a positive and friendly attitude. I have the ability to find solutions to problems and to resolve any issues arising with guests in a fast and efficient manner.

I have demonstrated skills and capabilities in:
- Managing day to day operations of all Food and Beverage outlets to deliver an excellent guest and team member experience
- Planning and controlling all areas of cost management pertaining to cost of food, beverages and other related expenses
- Planning and managing procurement, production and presentation of all food and beverages in the hotel in a safe, sanitary and cost effective manner to achieve a profitable result
- Ensuring that each customer receives outstanding service by providing a friendly and welcoming atmosphere
- Reviewing food service trends and suggesting modifications in menu and presentation
- Controlling food waste, product inventory, payroll and expenses

- Hiring, training, scheduling, supervising, motivating and evaluating staff
- Setting achievable goals, developing budgets, and monitoring revenues and expenditures
- Ensuring practice of health and safety regulations
- Ensuring compliance with all health and safety regulations and Company policies and procedures
- Acting as Hotel Manager once per month

My resume is attached which will provide you with more information about my skills and experience. I am confident that I will be an asset to your organization and look forward to working for you.

Thank you for taking the time to consider my application. I look forward to learning about the next steps in the selection process and can assure you that my drive, commitment and enthusiasm will be a great value to your team.

Sincerely,
Signature

Name

Appendix 2: Sample Resumes

Job: Administrative Officer

NAME

Street Address, City, Province, Postal Code

• Telephone Number   • Email address

CAREER OBJECTIVE: Management Position

SUMMARY OF QUALIFICATIONS

Versatile, confident and organized Operations Manager with over 10 years of administrative experience. High level of professionalism with ability to hand confidential information and act with discretion. Ability to work in a team environment and independently with little or no supervision. Strong interpersonal, time management and communication skills with the ability to take initiative. Sound judgment and problem solving skills with the ability to handle sensitive and non-routine issues in a high paced environment. Experienced with diverse clientele.

PROFESSIONAL EXPERIENCE

JOB TITLE   **2011 - present**
COMPANY NAME, CITY, PROVINCE, COUNTRY (If outside Canada)

- Oversee all business and highly confidential company matters including human resource management, vendor identification, procurement and management, facilities management, product purchasing and insurance, SEO, advertising, financial and accounting matters and legal compliance
- Supervise over 40 employees working at four different companies and two locations
- Prepare and monitor account balances of three sister

companies: *List 3 companies*

- Create and place 7 advertisements per day, handle 5-10 invoices per day and keep record of all pre-authorized payments
- Handle all matters pertaining to the Better Business Bureau and Consumer Protection office including customer complaints and release of relevant documents
- Purchased to date over 2000 vehicles on line at various auctions
- Organize all off-site sales including the organization of the sale facility, maintain Dealer Plates and secure all sales deposits in amounts ranging from $1000 to $200,000
- Developed, implemented and ensure compliance with company HR policies and procedures
- Reviewed and authorized to date over 2000 new loan applications and am Commissioner for Oaths
- Audited over 4000 files to ensure correct documentation and investigated audit defects
- Investigated and negotiated insurance claims and opened over 400 arbitration files
- Handled 7 Employment Standard cases and providing needed documents to authorities successfully achieving no penalties by the Employment Standards Branch
- Arranged and coordinated approximately 15 corporate events for staff and customers

JOB TITLE   2010 - 2011
COMPANY NAME, CITY, PROVINCE, COUNTRY (If outside Canada)

- Updated over 2500 conformation statements on Personal Property Registration
- Updated over 4000 credit reports to Trans Union of Canada and Equifax
- Prepared over 500 documents of transfer, 100 legal documents and 150 proof of claims for bankruptcies

- Performed clerical and administrative duties for Manager in sister company

JOB TITLE   **2007 - 2010**
COMPANY NAME, CITY, PROVINCE, COUNTRY (If outside Canada)

- Performed clerical duties including frontline reception
- Answered over 200 telephone calls per day from public
- Maintained records of daily attendance for 43 employees
- Greeted approximately 100 people daily and booked 5-10 daily appointments with clients
- Maintained inventory and ordered supplies form about 15 vendors

JOB TITLE   **2011 - present**
COMPANY NAME, CITY, PROVINCE, COUNTRY (If outside Canada)

- Provided support to 11-member sales team ensuring all sales and service objectives were met
- Maintained records of all orders, prepared invoices and prepared payment cheques
- Performed clerical duties including answering customer inquiries, problem solving, provision of new product information, training of new customer service representatives and development of new policies and procedures

LANGUAGES

Fluent in English, Hindi and Punjabi

COMPUTER SKILLS

Proficient in Microsoft Office Suite, Simply Accounting, database applications, electronic mail and Internet research
Keyboarding speed: 50 w.p.m.

EDUCATION

Masters Program in Business Administration, *Institution Name, Country, Year*
Bachelor of Arts (Accounting), *Institution Name, Country, Year*

PROFESSIONAL DEVELOPMENT

Training in WHMIS, Emergency First Aid and CPR

REFERENCES AVAILABLE ON REQUEST

Job: Finance

NAME
Street Address, City, Province, Postal Code
- Telephone Number
- Email address

SUMMARY OF QUALIFICATIONS

Twenty-one years of proven accounting management experience that emphasizes high productivity, efficiency, accuracy, ease-of-use and cost containment. Well-developed organizational, time management, communication and analytical skills with demonstrated problem-solving capabilities. Proven track record in achieving sound development and monitoring of budgets for grants, contracts and general funds. Familiar with a variety of accounting, finance, payroll and human resources concepts, practices and procedures. Self-motivating with the initiative and ability to multitask in a fast-paced environment with proven ability to work effectively to achieve agency objectives. Demonstrated experience working in a non-profit, unionized environment with the ability to work independently and as part of a team.

PROFESSIONAL EXPERIENCE

JOB TITLE   **1994 - present**
COMPANY NAME, CITY, PROVINCE, COUNTRY (If outside Canada)

Finance and Accounting

- Direct and control the operations of the accounting function and financial activities of *Name of Organization* including bookkeeping, payroll, deferred revenue and accounts receivable schedules, account reconciliation, cash flow, preparation of accounting and financial, narrative and statistical reports and statements, budget monitoring systems maintenance, resource and expense tracking systems, resolution of any escalated vendor disputes and billing charges, monitoring and analysis of general ledger account, preparation of annual audit documentation, and provision of financial support to directors and managers

- Develop and coordinate annual $10,000,000 budget preparation in conjunction with 18 managers and 8 program directors providing on-going financial information/recommendations throughout the fiscal year
- Contribute to and review 22 funding proposals and applications annually
- Analyze 13 project reports monthly and contributions/grant details, provide accurate financial information and advice to 9 program managers, process 13 monthly and 7 quarterly claims to funders, coordinate approval processes of 140 accounts payable invoices per month, rectify escalated accounts payable issues monthly from 10 employees and 5 vendors, code the general ledger and process vendor invoice payments ranging from $120 to $55,000
- Perform accurate billings and monthly posting to remediation accounts for $25,000 budget, deposit third party cheques of $500,000/month and monthly reserve transfers of $24,000, handle month end allocations including opening approximately 10 new accounts monthly, and conduct month-end balance sheet reviews, reconcile any variances and prepare month end financial statements for directors
- Coded the general ledger and processed 120 vendor invoice payments of $55,000

Supervisory Skills and Human Resources

- Train, coach, mentor and lead the work of a 3-person team
- Coordinate information flow regarding pay and benefits to 80 employees
- Maintain up-to-date knowledge and understanding of ever changing HR requirements, policies and procedures, labour standard laws and collective agreement

- Recommend corrective actions on accounting issues to Senior Managers
- Recruit and interview potential candidates for available accounting positions

Internal and External Client Engagement

- Clarify, coach and guide 8 directors and 18 managers on budgeting, invoicing, monthly financial updates and periodic financial reporting tasks
- Meet with 6 Department Heads to communicate financial information as needed
- Collaborate with 26 directors and managers to reconcile accounts ranging from $5,000 to $4,500,000
- Liaise with federal and provincial governments and 20 community agencies including *Name Agencies* on matters related to financial and administrative functions and concerns, billing matters and contract changes
- Produce and release financial information to 9 different funding agencies, 12 other organizations, and 22 external auditors

Facilities and Equipment Monitoring

- Monitor purchase of all agency capital assets totaling $75,000 and oversee assignment of assets to departments
- Monitor all leased equipment contract payments totaling $25,000 and balance and designate the fees according to program usage

Information Systems Management

- Implemented an information system, in conjunction with *Job Title* Interpretation Translation department, that was to be used on an interim basis prior to software purchase but remains in use till date due to its efficiency and effectiveness

Risk Prevention, Management and Accreditation

- Prepared all documentation for _Name Organization's_ agency accreditation in conjunction with the Executive Director and accounting team
- Participate in on-going risk prevention and management activities

COMPUTER SKILLS

Proficient in Accounting and Payroll software including AccPac-Sage, Pay@Work-ADP, ERP, and Simply accounting and Microsoft Office applications Access, Excel, Outlook, PowerPoint, Word and Windows XP Professional OS

LANGUAGES

Fluent in English and Spanish

EDUCATION

Diploma in computerized Accounting, _Institution Name, Country, Year_
Faculty of Business Administration, _Institution Name, Country, Year_

PROFESSIONAL DEVELOPMENT

Conflict Resolution Workshop, 2015
CIC Regulations and Ways to Make Proper Claims Webinar, 2014
Year-End Payroll Workshop, 2012
Government Changes Workshop, 2004
Communication Workshop, 2003
Year-End Payroll Workshop, 1994

REFERENCES UPON REQUEST

Job: Hospitality

NAME

Street Address, City, Province, Postal Code

• Telephone Number   • Email address

CAREER OBJECTIVE: FOOD AND BEVERAGE
MANAGER

SUMMARY OF QUALIFICATIONS

Proven manager with over seventeen years of hospitality experience in hotel food and beverage operation management, customer service and team management. Results-oriented with strong leadership and interpersonal skills; effective organizational, planning and communication skills; exceptional customer service skills; and excellent budgetary, projection and cost control skills ensuring the highest level of guest satisfaction at all times. Demonstrated ability to work under pressure in a fast-pace hotel environment while exceeding guest and company expectations. Self-motivating with the initiative and ability to multitask and oversee, supervise and train 90 staff in multiple hotel dining outlets.

PROFESSIONAL EXPERIENCE

JOB TITLE   **2012 - present**
COMPANY NAME, CITY, PROVINCE, COUNTRY (If outside Canada)

- Direct and oversee operations of 6 dining outlets with 350-seat capacity in 218-room 5 Star hotel forecasted to annually serve 369,000

- Hire, train, schedule, supervise, motivate, evaluate and lead team of 90 staff to maximize employee engagement, service and teamwork

- SMART START Develop and sustain personal contact with culinary team and in-room dining team to maintain high quality food and beverage offerings and impeccable presentation in line with hotel standards.
- Lead, guide and direct operations of each dining facility to maximize profitability and minimize operating costs
- Plan, direct and implement Food and Beverage strategic business plans •
- Prepare and monitor the annual Food and Beverage budgets and revenue forecasts pro-actively addressing trough periods•
- Analyze Profit and Loss statements and develop strategies for improvement and guest experience enhancements•
- Participate actively in the hotel community to further inter-departmental working relationships
- Acts as Hotel General Manager once per month demonstrating ability to apply technical, professional or product expertise to everyday hotel situations

JOB TITLE   2010 - 2012
COMPANY NAME, CITY, PROVINCE, COUNTRY (If outside Canada)

- Directed and oversaw operations of 150-seat capacity restaurant leading 28-member team
- Responsible for all revenues, expenditures and annual budget
- Introduced a minimum of one touch-point per quarter.
- Managed customer database to effectively market and promote restaurant products and services.
- Established guest service standards and monitored implementation to ensure target market needs were met.
- Conducted departmental orientation training for all new employees.

- Recruited prospective employees at Catering Colleges as part of hotel's recruitment strategy and interview panel member.

JOB TITLE   **2008 - 2010**
COMPANY NAME, CITY, PROVINCE, COUNTRY (If outside Canada)

- Directed and oversaw operations of 150-seat capacity restaurant leading 28-member team
- Improved guest satisfaction tracking system results from 76% to 89% consistently quarter to quarter during 2010-11

JOB TITLE   **2002 - 2008**
COMPANY NAME, CITY, PROVINCE, COUNTRY (If outside Canada)

- Directed and oversaw operations of 70-seat capacity lounge and bar leading a 8-member team
- Awarded *Best Manager* in 2009

LANGUAGES
Fluent in English and Hindi

COMPUTER SKILLS
Proficient in Windows, Triton, Opera and OnQ

EDUCATION
Masters in Tourism Management, *Institution Name, Country, Year*
Hotel Management Diploma, *Institution Name, Country, Year*

REFERENCE UPON REQUEST

Appendix 3: Soft Skills

The following table lists some of the Soft Skills Canadian employers look for:

Able to accept constructive criticism	Able to collaborate with others
Active listening	Adaptable
Appropriate and effective communicator	Assertive
Can deal with difficult people and situations	Can follow directions and regulations
Can establish interpersonal relationships	Can manage and resolve conflict effectively
Can work cooperatively with others	Can work independently with limited supervision
Critical thinker	Culturally competent
Decision maker	Delegator
Dependable	Diversity Awareness
Emotional Intelligence	Facilitation
Flexible	Friendly and courteous
Honest	Innovator
Interpersonal	Leadership
Logical	Manager of teams, meetings, staff
Mentor	Motivated and able to motivate others
Multi-tasker	Negotiator
Organizational	Planning
Positive work ethic	Presentation
Problem solver	Public speaker
Punctual	Reliable
Resilient	Respects deadlines

Respectful of others	Results oriented
Safety conscious	Self aware
Self directed	Strategic
Stress management	Takes initiative
Takes ownership	Team player
Understands appropriate nonverbal and verbal communication	Understands business etiquette
Willingness to continually learn	Works well under pressure
Work-Life balance	Writing skills

Appendix 4: Common Idioms and Terms

Terms and Idioms	Definition
Across the board	Something is applied to everyone equally
Actions speak louder than words	What a person actually does rather than what they say they will do
ASAP	As soon as possible
At the eleventh hour	Handing in assignments at the last minute
Biffy	Toilet
Bunnyhug (Saskatchewan)	Hooded pullover sweatshirt
Chesterfield	Sofa
Double-Double	A cup of coffee with two creams and two sugars
Downhomer	A resident of Newfoundland
Eh?	An interjection, similar to "you know?"
Face the music	Accept the consequences of your actions
Flea market	Outdoor shopping bazaar
FYI	For your information
Gameplan	Plan of action and a strategy to achieve goal
Give me a break	Give someone a chance
Grab a bite	Going to a restaurant to eat
Housecoat	Bathrobe
Hydro	Electricity
Icing on the cake	An extra bonus
I'm all ears	I am ready to listen
Islander	A person from Prince Edward Island
Jam buster (Manitoba)	Jelly doughnut
Keep your shirt on	Remain calm
Learn the ropes	Master the job
Long shot	Probability is small

Term and Idioms	Definition
Maritimer	A resident of the Maritime provinces
My lips are sealed	Will keep a secret and never tell
Mounties	Royal Canadian Mounted Police (RCMP)
Neck of the woods	A specific neighborhood or area where people live and common with
Nip in the bud	Stop a problem in the early stage
No strings attached	Do not have any obligations
On a shoestring	Living on very little money
Paint the town red	Going out and enjoying a night of entertainment
Part ways	Finished with a relationship either at work or personally
Pogie	Welfare; government assistance
Politically correct	Challenges vocabulary that implies prejudice, racism, sexism, homophobia
Pop	Bubbly soft drinks
Pulling your leg	Teasing or joking
Put it in a nutshell	Summarize it clearly
Raining cats and dogs	Very heavy rainfall
Red tape	Government bureaucracies that are time-consuming
R&R	Rest and relaxation
ROI	Return on investment
Rule of thumb	General guideline based on experience
Runners	Running shoes
Serviette	Napkin
Sneakers	Running shoes

Term and Idioms	Definition
Speak of the devil	Someone suddenly appear that you were discussing
Street dog (Toronto)	A hotdog in a bun sold by a street vendor
Take the ball and run	Move forward on an idea or new direction
Top brass	Most important senior people in an organization
Two-four	A 24-pack of beer
Walk in the park	Task or activity that is easy
Warts and all	Accepting a person's flaws
Water under the bridge	Put matter in the past

Common Jargon in Newfoundland and Labrador	Definition
Angishore	A weak, miserable person
Arn	Any
Bayman	Anyone not from St. John's
Bliver	To shiver with cold
Chucklehead	A stupid person
Clobber	An untidy state of things
Do you want some taken up	Want some supper
Duckish	Between sunset and dark
Gandy	Pancake
I just dies at you	You make me laugh
It's a mausey day	A foggy, wet day
Mind now	You do not really expect that
Mush	Porridge
Narn	None
Prog	Food
Stunned	Foolish or naive
Where's ya longs to	Where do you come from
Yer	Here

Bibliography

Banks Operating in Canada, Canadian Bankers Association, www.cba.ca/en/component/content/category/61-banks-operating-in-canada

Calgary Economic Development, http://www.calgaryeconomicdevelopment.com/industries

Canadian Immigrants, http://www.canadaimmigrants.com/immigration/statistics/

Canadian Association of Statutory Human Rights Agencies, Links, www.cashra.ca/links.html

Canadian Human Rights Act, http://www.chrc-ccdp.ca/eng/content/what-discrimination

Caring for Kids New to Canada, Canadian Paediatric Society, www.kidsnewtocanada.ca/mental-health/ptsd

Central Intelligence Agency, https://www.cia.gov

City Data, http://www.city-data.com/canada/Winnipeg-work.html

City of Fredericton, http://www.fredericton.ca/en/communityculture/communityprofile.asp

City of Ottawa, *Economy and Demographics*, http://ottawa.ca/en/long-range-financial-plans/long-range-financial-plan-iii-part-1-and-part-2/economy-and-demographics

City of Toronto, *Key Industry Sectors*, http://www1.toronto.ca/wps/portal/contentonly?vgnextoid=401132d0b6d1e310VgnVCM10000071d60f89RCRD

Constructive Criticism, Wikipedia, https://en.wikipedia.org/wiki/Constructive_criticism

Economic Development Brandon,
http://economicdevelopmentbrandon.com/industry-employment-business

eMentalHealth.ca ,
http://m.ementalhealth.ca/index.php?m=article&ID=8885&r=Winnipeg-Regional-Health-Authority

Employment and Social Development Canada,
http://srv129.services.gc.ca/ei_regions/eng/vancouv.aspx?rates=1

Employment and Social Development Canada,
http://srv129.services.gc.ca/ei_regions/eng/edmonton.aspx?rates=1

Employment and Social Development Canada,
http://srv129.services.gc.ca/ei_regions/eng/calgary.aspx?rates=1

Employment and Social Development Canada,
http://srv129.services.gc.ca/ei_regions/eng/winnipeg.aspx?rates=1

Employment and Social Development Canada,
http://srv129.services.gc.ca/ei_regions/eng/toronto.aspx?rates=1

Expatistan, *Cost of Living Index*, www.expatistan.com

Federal labour Standards, https://www.canada.ca/en/employment-social-development/programs/employment-standards.html

Found Locally, http://foundlocally.com/stjohns/Local/Info-CityInfo.htm

Government of Canada, *Labour Laws*:
http://www.labour.gc.ca/eng/home.shtml

HeretoHelp, BC Partners for Mental Health and Addictions Information,
http://www.heretohelp.bc.ca/visions/trauma-and-victimization-vol3/war-trauma-in-refugees

Housing in Canada, Citizenship and Immigration Canada, www.cic.gc.ca/english/newcomers/after-housing.asp

Immigration and Ethnocultural Diversity in Canada, Statistics Canada, www12.statcan.gc.ca/nhs-enm/2011/as-sa/99-010-x/99-010-x2011001-eng.cfm

Labour Force Characteristics, Population 15 and Older, by Census Metropolitan, Statistics Canada, www.statcan.gc.ca/tables-tableaux/sum- som/l01/cst01/labor35-eng.htm

Labour Force Characteristics, Unadjusted, by Census Metropolitan, Statistics Canada, www.statcan.gc.ca/tables-tableaux/sum-som/l01/cst01/lfss04k- eng.htm

Living in Canada, living in New Brunswick, http://www.livingin-canada.com/living-in-new-brunswick.html

MoneySense, http://www.moneysense.ca/canadas-best-places-to-live-2015-full-ranking/

National Average Price Map, The Canadian Real Estate Association, http://crea.ca/content/national-average-price-map

Office of the Superintendent of Financial Institutions, May 2014, http://www.osfi-bsif.gc.ca/eng/pages/default.aspx

Provincial Workplace Standards, http://www.cic.gc.ca/english/work/labour-standards.asp?_ga=1.16594995.429274252.1464188563

Population of Census Metropolitan Areas, Statistics Canada, www.statcan.gc.ca/tables-tableaux/sum-som/l01/cst01/demo05a-eng.htm

Population Density, The World Bank, http://data.worldbank.org/indicator/EN.POP.DNST

Provincial Workplace Standards:
www.esdc.gc.ca/en/jobs/workplace/index.page

Quebec International, http://www.quebecinternational.ca/key-industries

Sirin, Selcuk R. and Rogers-Sirin, Lauren, *The Educational and Mental Health Needs of Syrian Refugee Children*, Migration Policy Institute, October 2015

Statistics Canada, http://www12.statcan.gc.ca/nhs-enm/2011/as-sa/99-010-x/99-010-x2011001-eng.cfm

Statistics Canada, *Immigration and Ethnocultural Diversity in Canada*, http://www12.statcan.gc.ca/nhs-enm/2011/as-sa/99-010-x/99-010-x2011001-eng.cfm

Statistics Canada, *Labour Force Characteristics, Unemployment*, http://www5.statcan.gc.ca/cansim/a26?lang=eng&retrLang=eng&id=2820135&paSer=&pattern=&stByVal=1&p1=1&p2=37&tabMode=dataTable&csid

Statistics Canada, *Life Satisfaction Across Metropolitan Areas and Economic Regions in Canada*, http://www.statcan.gc.ca/pub/11-626-x/11-626-x2015046-eng.htm

Statistics Canada, *Median Total Income, by Family Type, By Census Metropolitan Areas*, http://www.statcan.gc.ca/tables-tableaux/sum-som/l01/cst01/famil107a-eng.htm

Statistics Canada, *Population of Census Metropolitan Areas*, http://www.statcan.gc.ca/tables-tableaux/sum-som/l01/cst01/demo05a-eng.htm

The Canadian Real Estate Association, *National Average Price Map*, http://crea.ca/content/national-average-price-map

The Canadian Trade Commissioner Service, *St. John's: An Emerging Economy and Cultural Capital*, http://www.international.gc.ca/investors-investisseurs/cities-villes/saint_johns.aspx?lang=eng

The City of Edmonton, *Industries*, http://www.edmonton.ca/business_economy/demographics_profiles/industries.aspx

The Old Farmer's Almanac, http://www.almanac.com/content/windchill-chart-canada

The WorldBank, http://data.worldbank.org/indicator/SP.POP.TOTL

Two small men with big hearts, http://twosmallmen.com/halifax-ns-movers/main-industries-and-job-opportunities-in-halifax

World Fact Book, Central Intelligence Agency, www.cia.gov/library/publications/resources/the-world-factbook/

What are Bridging Programs for Internationally-Trained Professionals and Tradespeople, Settlement.Org, http://settlement.org/ontario/employment/plan- my-career/job-skills-training/what-are-bridging-programs-for-internationally- trained-professionals-and-tradespeople/

Wikipedia, https://en.wikipedia.org/wiki/Constructive_criticism

Wind Chill - The Chilling Facts, Environment Canada, www.ec.gc.ca/meteo- weather/default.asp?lang=En&n=5FBF816A-1#table1

Workplace, Health and Safety, https://www.canada.ca/en/employment-social-development/programs/health-safety.html

World Health Organization, www.emro.who.int/jor/jordan-news/syrian-refugees.html

Index

About the Author

Barbara Dixon is the Senior Consultant and President of Diversity ERAA Training. She is recognized internationally as one of Canada's top diversity trainers and innovative leaders in immigrant integration programming. She has delivered workshops and keynote presentations to over 23,000 participants within 112 organizations across Canada and internationally. She is author of the *Newcomer's Guide to Canada* and the *Syrian Refugee Guide to Canada*.

Barbara envisioned and created Canada's first post-secondary institution's diversity and immigrant student support department, initiated and implemented the first Certificate Program in Canada to train certified intercultural trainers, established the first Centre for Immigrant and International Students at a Canadian college and started the first Mentor Program for Immigrants in Canada before it was even called mentoring.

Barbara developed the pre-arrival group orientation workshop for the Canadian Immigrant Integration Program (CIIP) for Federal Skilled Workers and provincial nominees from Manitoba, Saskatchewan and the East Coast provinces. She has travelled to 27 countries and has worked in Nigeria, India, China, Philippines and the UK.

Barbara is available to help you settle and integrate successfully in Canada. She is available to assist employers gain cultural competency skills and help newcomers integrate successfully into the workplace.

You can contact Barbara at: **diversityeraa@gmail.com** or through the Diversity ERAA website: **http://diversityeraa.ca**